LET'S EAT
English

LET'S
EAT
English

Editors
Wendy Hobson/Christine Smeeth

foulsham
LONDON • NEW YORK • TORONTO • SYDNEY

foulsham

Yeovil Road, Slough, Berkshire, SL1 4JH

ISBN 0-572-01832-0

Photoset in Great Britain by Encounter Photosetting, Fleet, Hampshire
Printed in Great Britain by Cox & Wyman Ltd., Reading

Contents

1. **Introduction** 6
   Notes on the Recipes 8
2. **Soups and Appetisers** 9
3. **Seafood** 24
4. **Poultry and Game** 38
5. **Beef** 54
6. **Lamb and Pork** 66
7. **Eggs and Cheese** 82
8. **Vegetables and Pulses** 92
9. **Desserts** 106
10. **Cakes and Biscuits** 122
11. **Sauces and Dressings** 134
12. **Preserves and Drinks** 146

Index 155

Introduction

As our tastes become wider and the opportunities for tasting and enjoying foods from all over the world become greater, we can sometimes neglect the traditional English dishes which we have enjoyed for generations.

English cooking is not just about fish and chips – although beautifully cooked fresh fish makes a wonderful meal! There is a whole range of tasty and tempting meals making use of all kinds of meat and fish, not to mention the range of wonderful cheeses and vegetables available.

Cooking methods vary from the quickly fried, the grilled and baked, to the long, slow tenderising cooking of a hearty stew or casserole. Complicated techniques and fiddly preparation do not need to feature in traditional English cookery. You can enjoy simply-prepared, delicious meals which are easy for any busy cook to fit into their schedule.

The many vegetable dishes can serve as meals in themselves or to complement a meat dish. Gone are the days when vegetables were boiled out of any vestige of flavour or texture! We have learnt to cook vegetables simply so that they retain their optimum flavour and just that tiny hint of crunch which makes them so healthy and delicious.

Desserts are a speciality of English cookery, as no one can beat a traditional pudding – whether it be a hot date steamed pudding with rum sauce for a winter day, or a delicate summer pudding, lightly chilled, to round off a summer meal. Using the fruits of the season or the many dried ingredients available throughout the year, you can make wonderful puddings for family or friends in the best English tradition.

Traditional tea-time should not be forgotten, either, as cakes, both small and large, come in all shapes and sizes from the best English kitchens to savour with your afternoon tea or supper.

While we all enjoy the opportunity of bringing an international flavour into our kitchens, let's not lose that wonderful English tradition.

Notes on the Recipes

1. Follow one set of measurements only, do not mix metric and Imperial.

2. Eggs are size 2.

3. Wash fresh produce before preparation.

4. Spoon measurements are level.

5. Adjust seasoning and strongly-flavoured ingredients, such as onions and garlic, to suit your own taste.

6. If you substitute dried for fresh herbs, use only half the amount specified.

Soups and Appetisers

*Warming soups make a wonderful entrée
to a winter dinner, or a tasty and
nutritious lunch served with crusty bread
and some grated cheese. They can be made
with almost any combination of
ingredients, and with a little forethought
are no trouble to make. They freeze well,
too, so you can always have your own
soups ready.*

*If you prefer a different appetiser for your
meal, there are plenty of other alternatives
in the range of English cuisine.*

1 Cock-a-Leekie Soup

Ingredients

15 ml/1 tbsp butter or margarine
225 g/8 oz chicken breast
350 g/12 oz leeks
1.2 l/2 pts/5 cups chicken stock
1 bouquet garni
Salt and freshly ground black pepper

Method

1. Melt the butter or margarine and fry the chicken until golden brown on both sides.

2. Cut the white parts of the leeks in quarters lengthways then chop into 2.5 cm/1 in pieces. Reserve the green parts. Add the white parts to the pan and fry for 5 minutes until soft.

3. Add the stock and bouquet garni and season with salt and pepper. Bring to the boil, cover and simmer for 30 minutes until the chicken is tender.

4. Remove the chicken, discard the skin and bones and cut into large chunks. Arrange the chicken in a warmed serving bowl and pour over the hot soup.

Serves 4

2 | Oxtail Soup

Ingredients

50 g/2 oz/¼ cup lard
1 oxtail, jointed
1 onion, chopped
2 carrots, chopped
1.2 l/2 pts/5 cups beef stock
6 peppercorns
salt and freshly ground black pepper
5 ml/1 tsp lemon juice
15 ml/1 tbsp plain flour (optional)

Method

1. Melt the lard and fry the oxtail until lightly browned then transfer the joints to a large saucepan. Add the onion and carrots to the lard and fry until lightly browned.

2. Transfer the vegetables to the saucepan with the stock and peppercorns and bring to the boil. Cover and simmer gently for 5 hours.

3. Strain the soup and skim off the fat. Return to the pan, season with salt, pepper and lemon juice and reheat.

4. If necessary, mix the flour with a little cold water then stir it into the soup and simmer until the soup thickens slightly.

Serves 4

3 | Pea and Ham Soup

Ingredients

> 15 ml/1 tbsp butter or margarine
> 1 onion, finely chopped
> 1 potato, diced
> 350 g/12 oz frozen peas
> 1.2 l/2 pts/5 cups chicken stock
> 100 g/4 oz cooked ham, shredded
> Salt and freshly ground black pepper
> 60 ml/4 tbsp single cream

Method

1. Melt the butter and fry the onion and potato gently for about 10 minutes until soft but not browned.

2. Add the peas, stock and half the ham and season with salt and pepper. Bring to the boil and simmer gently for 15 minutes.

3. Purée the soup in a food processor or blender then rub it through a sieve back into a clean pan.

4. Add the remaining ham to the soup and reheat gently without allowing the soup to boil. Stir in the cream and season to taste with salt and pepper.

Serves 4

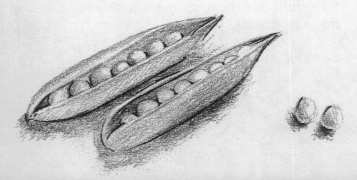

Tomato and Barley Soup

Ingredients

30 ml/2 tbsp butter or margarine
1 onion, chopped
1 carrot, chopped
1 stalk celery, chopped
450 g/1 lb tomatoes, skinned and quartered
25 g/1 oz crushed barley
900 ml/1½ pts/3¾ cups chicken stock
1 bouquet garni
Salt and freshly ground black pepper
30 ml/2 tbsp cream

Method

1. Melt the butter or margarine in a large saucepan and fry the onion, carrot and celery until softened. Add the tomatoes, barley, stock and bouquet garni, bring to the boil, cover and simmer for 45 minutes.

2. Remove the bouquet garni and season to taste with salt and pepper. Purée in a food processor or blender then rub through a sieve back into the pan.

3. Reheat the soup gently and swirl in the cream just before serving.

Serves 4

5 Winter Vegetable Soup

Ingredients

15 ml/1 tbsp oil
1 onion, sliced
1 clove garlic, crushed
1 potato, diced
1 carrot, sliced
1 leek, sliced
1 stalk celery, chopped
45 ml/3 tbsp sherry
900 ml/1½ pts/3¾ cups chicken stock
5 ml/1 tsp mixed herbs
Salt and freshly ground black pepper

Method

1. Heat the oil in a large saucepan and fry the onion and garlic until softened. Add the potato, carrot, leek and celery and stir until coated with oil.

2. Add the sherry, stock and herbs and season with salt and pepper. Bring to the boil, cover and simmer for 25 minutes. Serve hot with grated cheese, fresh bread or croûtons.

Serves 4

6 English Pottage

Invented, as far as is known, by Sir Kenelm Digby (1603-65) and revived regularly since that time, English Pottage has grown over the years into a hearty, filling main course soup.

Ingredients

900 ml/1½ pts/3¾ cups chicken stock
1.25 kg/2½ lb chicken
Yolks of 4 eggs
150 ml/¼ pt/⅔ cup white wine
½ teaspoon nutmeg
150 ml/¼ pt cream
2 large onions, roughly chopped
450 g/1 lb white endive (chicory)
50 g/2 oz crushed barley
Large bunch fresh herbs
Salt and pepper

Method

1. Put the chicken into a large saucepan and pour over the stock. Add the herbs, barley, nutmeg and the chopped onions. Season with the salt and pepper. Bring to the boil and simmer for 45 minutes.

2. Wash the endive and cut into small chunks. Poach gently in boiled salted water for 20 minutes. Drain and keep hot.

3. Lift the chicken from the gravy and lay on a large plate. Remove the herbs. Beat the eggs and wine together and pour into the gently simmering gravy, stirring all the time. Continue stirring for 2-3 minutes until it forms a creamy consistency. Do not allow to boil. Blend in the cream.

4. Pour the gravy over the chicken. Spoon the chopped endive around the chicken and serve at once.

Serves 4

7 | Rabbit Soup

Ingredients

1 rabbit, jointed
2 large onions
5 ml/1 tsp ground cloves
Large bunch of herbs
50g /2 oz/¼ cup butter
50 g/2 oz/½ cup flour
1.2 l/2 pts/5 cups water

Method

1. Put the rabbit pieces into a large saucepan and cover with the water. Cut the onions in half and add to the pan with the herbs and salt and pepper. Simmer for 2 hours until the rabbit is tender.

2. Remove the meat from the bones and put into a blender with the remaining liquid and vegetables from the saucepan. Blend until smooth.

3. Heat the butter in a saucepan and gradually work in the flour. Mix in the ground cloves and pour in the soup. Simmer until the flour has disappeared and the soup has thickened.

Serves 6

8 | Two-Cheese Pots

Ingredients

50 g/2 oz *Double Gloucester cheese, grated*
50 g/2 oz *Cheshire cheese, grated*
60 ml/4 tbsp *single cream*
50 g/2 oz *cooked ham, finely chopped*
50 g/2 oz *fresh wholemeal breadcrumbs*
5 ml/1 tsp *Worcestershire sauce*
Pinch of mixed spice
Salt and freshly ground black pepper
2 *eggs, separated*

Method

1. Beat together the cheeses, cream, ham, breadcrumbs, Worcestershire sauce and spice. Season with salt and pepper. Beat the egg yolks into the mixture.

2. Whisk the egg whites until stiff then gently fold them into the mixture.

3. Spoon into greased ramekin dishes, stand them on a baking sheet and bake in a preheated oven at 200°C/400°F/gas mark 6 for about 15 minutes until well risen and golden brown. Serve at once.

Serves 4

9 | Buttered Mussels

Mussels have always been in abundance round the English coast. This recipe has been around since the sixteenth century, although mainly used as an hors-d'oeuvre or supper dish today. The delicious, fresh mussels and sweet smelling oven-baked rolls can be served with new boiled potatoes and a green salad for a more substantial meal.

Ingredients

6 large crusty rolls
12 cooked and shelled mussels per person (kept warm in some of the stock)
25 g/1 oz/¼ cup flour
75 g/3 oz/⅔ cup butter
300 ml/½ pt/1¼ cups milk
Pinch of nutmeg
Salt and pepper
Watercress to garnish

Method

1. Slice a small top from each roll and butter the insides. Brush a little melted butter over the outside of each roll.

2. Heat the remaining butter and stir in the flour. Cook for 1 minute and gradually blend in the milk. Season with the salt, pepper and nutmeg and continue stirring until the sauce thickens.

3. Drain the mussels and add to the sauce. Fill the rolls with this mixture. Bake in the oven at 325°F/160°C/gas mark 3 for 10 minutes. Garnish with the watercress and serve at once.

Serves 6

10 | Angels on Horseback

Oysters are a traditional part of the English heritage and although expensive to purchase today they were once considered 'a poor man's food'. Try this quick to prepare dish for special occasions.

Ingredients

6 slices bread
6 oysters
3 rashers streaky bacon
50 g/2 oz/¼ cup butter
15 ml/1 tbsp chopped parsley
Pepper

Method

1. Remove the crusts from the bread and fry in the butter. Keep warm.

2. Clean the beards from the oysters and sprinkle with the freshly ground pepper. Cut each rasher in half and run the blade of the knife along each slice to stretch it a little. Roll the oyster in the bacon and secure with a cocktail stick.

3. Fry the oyster for about 2-3 minutes in the butter, turning regularly. Do not allow to overcook. Place one oyster roll on each piece of fried bread and garnish with the chopped parsley. Serve immediately.

Serves 6

11 | Soft Roes with Bacon

This is a tasty recipe for a supper dish served with hot toast or for a more substantial meal it can be served with boiled potatoes and a hot vegetable. Roes are not used in today's cookery as often as they once were but this is an unusual dish needing little effort and well worth trying.

Ingredients

8 soft roes
100 g/4 oz/½ cup butter
75 g/3 oz fresh breadcrumbs
30 ml/2 tbsps chopped parsley
4 bacon rashers
10 ml/2 tsps lemon juice
3 shallots
Salt and pepper

Method

1. Butter an ovenproof dish. Lay the roes in a frying pan and season with salt and pepper. Cover with boiling water. Poach for 3-4 minutes, drain and lay in the buttered dish.

2. Chop the bacon and sprinkle over the roes. Mix the breadcrumbs with one tablespoon of the parsley and cover the bacon and roes. Place small pieces of butter over the breadcrumbs reserving the rest of the butter for the sauce. Bake at 400°F/200°C/gas mark 6 for 12-15 minutes until the breadcrumbs are brown.

3. Chop the shallots, finely, and fry with the remaining butter. Season with the remaining parsley, salt and pepper. Immediately before serving, stir in the lemon juice and pour over the browned top of the roes.

Serves 4

12 Watercress Soup

Ingredients

Large bunch watercress, washed
1 small onion, chopped
400ml/14 fl oz/1¾ cups stock
350g/12 oz potatoes, peeled and diced
Salt and pepper
2 egg yolks
60ml/4 tbsp single cream

Method

1. Chop the watercress reserving a few sprigs.

2. Peel and dice potatoes, place in a pan with the watercress, onion and stock and bring to the boil. Simmer for 20 minutes. Liquidise, retum to the pan and bring to the boil. Season well. Beat the egg yolks and cream together and stir into the soup. Garnish with the watercress sprigs.

Serves 4

13 | Devilled Ham Toasts

Hot, spicy and quick to make, this dish can be served as a starter or as a speedy snack for a lunchtime meal.

Ingredients

75 g/3 oz lean cooked ham, finely chopped
3 lean bacon rashers, chopped
10 ml/2 tsps Worcestershire sauce
Pinch of cayenne pepper
5 ml/1 tsp ready-made mustard
30 ml/2 tbsp butter
4 slices buttered toast
15 ml/1 tbsp finely chopped parsley

Method

1. Put the butter into a frying pan and cook the chopped bacon rashers until they are just turning brown. Mix in the ham, Worcestershire sauce, cayenne and mustard.

2. Cut a circle from each slice of bread with a cookie cutter and lay on individual plates.

3. Pile the mixture on to the circles of toast and serve immediately, sprinkled with the parsley.

Serves 4

14 | Whitebait

Ingredients

675 g/1½ lb whitebait
75 g/3 oz flour
Salt and pepper
Oil for frying
Cayenne pepper
15 ml/1 tbsp chopped parsley
Lemon

Method

1. Wash the whitebait and dry them carefully in a tea towel. Mix the flour with the salt and pepper. Shake the flour over them while they are still in the cloth, until they are all covered.

2. Heat the oil until hot and almost smoking and quickly fry the whitebait for 1 minute. Remove from the oil and drain. Heat the oil until it is smoking and dip the fish again for a further 1 minute until golden brown. This second frying will ensure they are crisp on the outside. Remove and drain.

3. Sprinkle with a little cayenne pepper and the chopped parsley. Serve with the lemon cut into four wedges.

Serves 4

Seafood

*With the ever-increasing interest
in a lighter, more healthy diet,
fish is returning to popularity.
Make use of the widening range
of fish available to add variety
and interest to your cooking.*

1 Crab Salad

Crab Salad is a long standing tradition of the West Country and coastal areas of England and has been a firm favourite with holiday-makers in more recent years.

Ingredients

450 g/1 lb crab meat
175 g/6 oz fresh breadcrumbs
30 ml/2 tsp wine vinegar
2.5 ml/½ tsp dry mustard
5 ml/1 tsp Worcestershire sauce
30 ml/2 tbsp butter
100 ml/3½ fl oz white sauce
Salt and pepper

Method

1. Clean the crab shells once the meat has been removed.

2. Mix together the crab meat, vinegar, mustard, Worcestershire sauce, white sauce and half the butter. Pack into the crab shells.

3. Top with the breadcrumbs and dot with the remaining butter.

4. Bake in the oven at 400°F/200°C/gas mark 6 for 20-25 minutes until brown on the surface. Serve at once.

Serves 3

2 Grilled Lobster

The epitome of luxury and has been for many years,
lobsters were once plentiful and made an elaborate dish.
They can be served with a creamy white or cheese sauce
laced with brandy and quickly grilled for an elegant supper
dish and look wonderful in a cool, dressed salad.

Ingredients

> 1 large lobster
> 75 g/3 oz/⅔ cup unsalted butter
> Juice of 1 lemon
> Black pepper

Method

1. Cut the lobster if half lengthways and remove the black or greenish sac from the head and the black or green thread which runs the length of the body.

2. Place the lobster on an ovenproof tray and season with the pepper. Put small pieces of butter over the flesh and cook under a hot grill for 10-15 minutes.

3. Pour over the lemon juice and serve at once.

Serves 2

3 Kedgeree

Ingredients

175 g/6 oz smoked haddock
175 g/6 oz haddock
350 g/12 oz long-grain rice
5 ml/1 tsp lemon juice
50 g/2 oz/¼ cup butter or margarine, melted
2 hard-boiled eggs, coarsely chopped
150 ml/¼ pt/⅔ cup single cream
Salt and freshly ground black pepper
30 ml/2 tbsp chopped fresh parsley

Method

1. Place the smoked haddock and haddock in a pan and just cover with water. Bring to the boil and simmer gently for 10 minutes.

2. Strain the cooking liquor on to the rice in a saucepan. Top up the liquid with water until it is 2.5 cm/1 in above the level of the rice, add the lemon juice, bring to the boil, cover and simmer for about 10 minutes until the rice is tender.

3. Remove the bones and skin and flake the fish. Keep it warm.

4. Drain the cooked rice and transfer to an ovenproof dish. Cook in a preheated oven at 150°C/300°F/ gas mark 2 for 5 minutes to dry out. Gently heat the cream until almost boiling.

5. Stir the fish, butter or margarine, most of the eggs and the cream into the rice. Season to taste with salt and pepper and serve sprinkled with the remaining eggs and parsley.

Serves 4

4 Tomato Fish Pie

Ingredients

450 g/1 lb cod or other white fish, skinned
50 g/2 oz fresh breadcrumbs
50 g/2 oz Cheddar cheese, grated
1 onion, chopped
2.5 ml/½ tsp mixed herbs
salt and freshly ground black pepper
300 ml/½ pt/1¼ cups milk
30 ml/2 tbsp butter or margarine
50 g/2 oz mushrooms, sliced
25 g/1 oz/¼ cup plain flour
30 ml/2 tbsp tomato purée
5 ml/1 tsp lemon juice
2.5 ml/½ tsp sugar
450 g/1 lb potatoes
2 sprigs watercress, chopped

Method

1. Arrange half the cod on the base of a greased shallow flameproof dish.

2. Mix together the breadcrumbs, cheese, onion and herbs and season with salt and pepper. Bind with a little milk, spoon over the fish and top with the remaining fish.

3. Melt the butter or margarine and fry the mushrooms for 2 minutes.

4. Add the flour and cook for 30 seconds, stirring. Add the remaining milk, the tomato purée, lemon juice and sugar and bring to the boil, stirring continuously. Simmer, stirring, for 2 minutes then pour over the fish.

5. Bake in a preheated oven at 190°C/375°F/gas mark 5 for 20 minutes.

6. Meanwhile, cook the potatoes in boiling water until tender then drain and mash. Spoon or pipe a border of mashed potato around the dish and return it to the oven for about 10 minutes until lightly browned. Serve garnished with watercress.

Serves 4

5 | Crab Pie

Crabs are not used as much as they once were and are considered time consuming and expensive however, in practice it takes only a few minutes to remove the crab from the shell and crab is not as expensive as many other types of fish compared with the quantity used in each recipe.

Ingredients

2 crabs
75 g/3 oz breadcrumbs
30 ml/2 tbsp butter
2.5 ml/½ tsp nutmeg
2.5 ml/½ tsp vinegar
Thinly sliced bread and butter
Salt and pepper

Method

1. Remove the crab meat from the shells and place in a bowl. Season with the nutmeg, breadcrumbs, salt and pepper. Place the fish back in the shells.

2. Heat the butter and stir in the vinegar. Pour over the fish and grill until brown.

3. Serve at once with the sliced bread and butter.

Serves 4

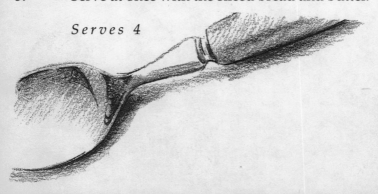

6 | Herrings in Oatmeal

Ingredients

4 medium herring
Salt and freshly ground black pepper
1 egg, beaten
75 g/3 oz medium oatmeal
15 ml/1 tbsp butter or margarine
15 ml/1 tbsp oil
1 lemon, cut into wedges

Method

1. Clean the fish and remove the heads and tails. To remove the backbone, place the fish on a board, cut side down, and press gently down the centre back. Turn over and ease out the backbone. Season the fish well with salt and pepper.

2. Dip the herring in egg then in oatmeal, pressing the oatmeal so that it is well covered.

3. Heat the butter or margarine and oil and fry the herrings for about 5 minutes on each side until cooked through and golden brown. Drain well and serve garnished with lemon wedges.

Serves 4

Steamed Sole in Cheese Sauce

This recipe is a traditional way of serving sole and gets away from that grilled or fried method that has become so well used. The sauce can be quickly made or if time is really short a ready-prepared variety can be used instead. To add a piquant flavour a few chopped capers can be sprinkled into the sauce just before serving.

Ingredients

> *4 Sole*
> *100 g/4 oz grated cheese*
> *50 g/2 oz/½ cup flour*
> *50 g/2 oz/¼ cup butter*
> *300 ml /½ pt/1¼ cups milk*
> *450 ml/¾ pt/2 cups stock*
> *1 wineglass white wine*
> *1 small onion, sliced*
> *1 carrot, chopped*
> *Large bunch of mixed herbs*
> *Salt and pepper*

Method

1. Trim the sole and add trimmings to the stock with the onion, carrot and chopped herbs. Season with the salt and pepper and bring to the boil. Lower the heat and simmer for 5 minutes adding the wine. Strain.

2. Lay the soles in the stock and poach for 15 minutes.

3. Heat the butter in a saucepan and stir in the flour. Gradually blend in the milk and cook until the sauce thickens, Stir in the grated cheese, reserving a little and season with the salt and pepper.

4. Drain the soles and lay on an ovenproof dish. Cover with the cheese sauce. Sprinkle over the remaining cheese and grill until lightly browned. Serve at once.

Serves 4

8 | Seafood Flan

Ingredients

6 oz shortcrust pastry
100 g/4 oz/ peeled prawns
100 g/4 oz cooked white fish
150 ml/¼ pint/⅔ cup single cream
15 ml/1 tbsp chopped parsley
2 eggs, beaten
Salt and Pepper

Method

1. Line flan tin with the pastry and bake blind for 10 minutes at 200°C/400°F/gas mark 6.

2. Flake the fish and chop the prawns and place in the pastry case. Beat the eggs, cream, parsley, salt and pepper and pour over the fish. Bake at 180°C/350°F/gas mark 4 for 25 minutes.

Serves 4-6

9 | Mussels with Saffron

Mussels have been collected around the coast of England since the Stone Age and eaten in various ways for both starters and main meals.

Ingredients

1.5 kg/3 lb mussels
600 ml/1 pt/2½ cups fish stock
1 glass white wine
3 shallots, finely chopped
2 carrots, cut into thin strips
2 leeks, cut into thin strips
1 stick celery, chopped into small pieces
Large pinch saffron
Grated rind and juice of 1 lemon
Salt and pepper
150 ml/¼ pt/¾ cup cream

Method

1.   Clean the mussels and remove the beards. Discard any which are open. Place the unopened mussels in a large saucepan with the fish stock, wine and chopped shallots. Cover the saucepan and cook over a high heat until all the mussels have opened.

2.   Drain the mussels. Strain the liquid back into the saucepan and cook over a high heat until the liquid reduces by half. Add the carrots, leeks and celery and continue cooking for 2 minutes. Remove from the heat.

3.   Stir in the cream, saffron, rind and juice of the lemon. Bring to the boil.

4. Remove the mussels from their shells and stir into the sauce. Season with the salt and pepper and serve in small dishes with chunks of crusty bread.

Serves 4-6

10 Lemon Fish Casserole

Ingredients

450g/1 lb white fish, skinned and boned
1 lemon
50 g/2 oz/¼ cup butter
Salt and pepper

Method

1. Cut the fish into four portions and put into a greased casserole dish. Season.

2. Cut the lemon into thin slices and place on top of the fish. Add the butter, cut in pieces and bake, covered, at 180°C/350°F/gas mark 4 for 30 minutes. Drain off the liquid to use as a sauce and serve at once.

Serves 4

11 Baked Mackerel with Mustard

Ingredients

4 mackerel
15 ml/1 tbsp plain flour
15 ml/1 tbsp mustard
30 ml/2 tbsp white wine vinegar
30 ml/2 tbsp water
15 ml/1 tbsp butter or margarine
Salt and freshly ground black pepper

Method

1. Clean the fish and dust them lightly with flour. Lay them side by side in a shallow, greased ovenproof dish.

2. Mix together the mustard, wine vinegar and water and pour over the fish. Dot with the butter or margarine and season with salt and pepper.

3. Cover and bake in a preheated oven at 190°C/375°F/gas mark 5 for about 30 minutes until tender, basting occasionally with the juices.

Serves 4

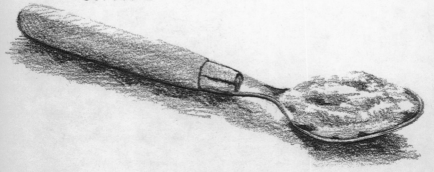

12 Eel and Green Peas

Ingredients

675 g/1½ lb eel
175 g/6 oz bacon
450 g/1 lb shelled peas
300 ml/½ pt/1¼ cups stock
6 large tomatoes
Pinch sugar
Bay leaf
1 onion, chopped
Salt and pepper

Method

1. Cut the bacon into small pieces and fry for 2 minutes. Add the chopped onion and continue cooking for a further 3-4 minutes.

2. Add the sliced eel to the bacon and onion and cook until lightly browned.

3. Chop the tomatoes and add to the eel and bacon mixture with the bay leaf, sugar and stock. Stir in the peas and simmer for 20 minutes.

Serves 4-6

Poultry and Game

*Chicken provides a range of tasty
and economical dishes and is
becoming increasingly popular
as we move towards a lower fat,
healthier diet. For the best
flavour, choose free-range or
corn-fed chickens.*

1 Gardener's Chicken

Ingredients

75 g/3 oz/⅓ cup unsalted butter
75 g/3 oz bacon, rinded and chopped
3 onions, sliced
2 stalks celery, chopped
100 g/4 oz mushrooms, sliced
4 chicken portions
450 g/1 lb new potatoes
225 g/8 oz turnips, sliced
400 g/14 oz canned tomatoes, drained
1 bouquet garni
salt and freshly ground black pepper
30 ml/2 tbsp grated orange rind
30 ml/2 tbsp chopped fresh parsley

Method

1. Melt the butter and fry the bacon, onions, celery and mushrooms until softened. Remove from the pan with a slotted spoon and place in a large ovenproof dish.

2. Fry the chicken in the butter until golden brown then arrange on the vegetables. Add the potatoes, turnips, tomatoes and bouquet garni and season with salt and pepper.

3. Cover and bake in a preheated oven at 150°C/300°F/gas mark 2 for about 1½ hours until the chicken is tender.

4. Mix together the orange rind and parsley and sprinkle over the casserole before serving.

Serves 4

2 Chicken with Leek and Watercress Sauce

Ingredients

4 chicken breasts, skinned
2 cloves garlic, sliced
30 ml/2 tbsp butter or margarine
3 leeks, finely chopped
2 shallots, chopped
1 bunch watercress
30 ml/2 tbsp port
300 ml/½ pt/1¼ cups chicken stock
2 egg yolks
75 ml/5 tbsp double cream

Method

1. Make small incisions into the chicken breasts and insert the slices of garlic.

2. Heat the butter or margarine and fry the leeks and shallots until soft but not browned. Reserve 2 sprigs of watercress and add the remainder with the port and stock. Bring to the boil and simmer for 10 minutes.

3. Add the chicken, cover and simmer for 20 minutes or until cooked through and tender. Transfer the chicken to a warmed serving plate.

4. Increase the heat under the sauce and boil until reduced slightly. Purée the sauce then return to a clean pan and bring almost to boiling.

5. Finely chop the remaining watercress and add it to the sauce.

6.   Mix together the egg yolks and cream. Mix in a little of the hot sauce, then stir the mixture into the sauce, taking care not to let the mixture boil. Stir over a low heat until the sauce thickens. Spoon over the chicken and serve at once.

Serves 4

3 | Roast Hare

Ingredients

1 hare, skinned and dried
25 g/1 oz/¼ cup flour
75 g/3 oz/⅔ cup butter
75 ml/5 tbsp stock
225 ml/8 fl oz/1 cup white wine
75 ml/5 tbsp double cream
Salt and pepper

Method

1.   Lightly flour the meat tin with half of the flour. Baste the hare with the butter. Place in the oven at 230°C/450°F/gas mark 8 for 15 minutes.

2.   Sprinkle with salt and pepper. Pour in the stock and white wine. Baste with the cream and bake at 200°C/400°F/gas mark 6 for 20 minutes.

Serves 4 - 6

Chicken with Parsley Dumplings

Ingredients

30 ml/2 tbsp oil
4 chicken portions
2 onions, sliced
2 cloves garlic, crushed
30 ml/2 tbsp plain flour
600 ml/1 pt/2½ cups chicken stock
1 bay leaf
10 ml/2 tsp mixed herbs
Salt and freshly ground black pepper
100 g/4 oz/1 cup self-raising flour
50 g/2 oz shredded suet
30 ml/2 tbsp chopped fresh parsley
1 egg, beaten

Method

1.   Heat the oil and fry the chicken until browned on all sides then transfer to a casserole dish. Add the onions and garlic to the pan and fry until soft but not browned then add them to the casserole.

2.   Stir the flour into the pan and cook for 1 minute, stirring. Stir in the stock, bring to the boil and simmer, stirring, until the sauce thickens. Add the bay leaf and herbs and season to taste with salt and pepper. Pour over the chicken, cover and bake in a preheated oven at 180°C/350°F/gas mark 4 for 1 hour.

3. Mix the flour, suet and parsley together with the egg. Roll into small dumplings, using floured hands, and add to the casserole. Cook, uncovered, for a further 30 minutes. Discard the bay leaf before serving.

Serves 4

5 Jugged Hare

A popular dish in England throughout the ages and
nowadays accompanied by stuffing balls and red currant
jelly.

Ingredients

1 hare (or rabbit)
1.2 l/2 pts/5 cups thick stock
2 large onions
8 cloves
50 g/2 oz/¼ cup butter
25 g/1 oz/¼ cup flour
2 glasses port wine
1 bayleaf
Bunch of herbs
Salt and pepper

Method

1.   Joint the hare and cook in a frying pan in the butter
     until brown. Season with the salt and pepper. Place
     in a casserole dish with the herbs, bayleaf and
     stock. Reserve the juices in the frying pan.

2.   Pierce the onions with the cloves and add to the
     stock. Cook, covered, in the oven at 350°F/180°C/gas
     mark 4 for 2 hours. Remove the bayleaf and herbs.

3.   Add the flour to the juices in the frying pan and
     cook for 1 minute. Blend in some of the stock from
     the casserole dish and cook until thickened. Add
     the glasses of wine. Stir this mixture into the stock
     in the casserole to thicken it and return to the oven
     without the lid for 1 hour or until required.

Serves 4.

6 Chicken and Stilton Rolls

Ingredients

4 chicken breasts, skinned
100 g/4 oz Stilton cheese, grated
75 g/3 oz/⅓ cup butter or margarine
8 rashers smoked back bacon, rinded
30 ml/2 tbsp oil
150 ml/¼ pt/⅔ cup red wine
150 ml/¼ pt/⅔ cup chicken stock
Salt and freshly ground black pepper
5 ml/1 tsp cornflour
Few sprigs watercress

Method

1. Slice the chicken breasts in half horizontally and beat the pieces flat.

2. Beat the cheese with the butter or margarine until soft then spread it over the chicken breasts. Roll them up, wrap in bacon and secure with cocktail sticks.

3. Heat the oil and fry the chicken rolls until lightly browned on all sides. Add the wine and stock, bring to the boil, cover and simmer gently for 35 minutes, turning occasionally, until the chicken is cooked through and tender.

4. Transfer the chicken to a warmed serving plate and remove the cocktail sticks. Mix the cornflour with a little water, stir it into the pan and simmer, stirring, until the sauce thickens. Pour over the chicken and serve garnished with watercress.

Serves 4

7 | Duck in Port

This is an early nineteenth-century recipe said to have come originally from the Gloucestershire area. A rich tasting meat but with the added flavours of port and spicy apples it makes a delicious meal for festive occasions.

Ingredients

> 1 duck
> 8 cooking apples
> 4 cloves
> ½ bottle port
> 300ml/½ pt/1¼ cups stock
> 25 g/1 oz/¼ cup flour
> 30 ml/2 tbsp butter
> Salt and pepper

Method

1. Peel and core the apples and place in a large bowl. Cover with the port and put a plate over the top. Tightly cover with foil and leave to marinate for 24 hours if possible.

2. Season the flour and rub over the surface of the duck. Place the duck in a baking tray with the butter and cook for 30 minutes at 400°F/200°C/gas mark 6.

3. Drain the fruit and heat the wine in a saucepan. Baste the duck with the wine. Put the apples around the duck with the cloves. Pour over the stock and continue to cook, basting every 15 minutes with the juices in the pan until the duck is cooked.

4. Remove the cloves and serve with the apples. The gravy may be thickened with a little cornflour if necessary.

Serves 4-6

8 | Spicy Chicken

Ingredients

6 chicken joints
30 ml/2 tbsp oil
5 ml/l tsp chilli powder
1 onion, chopped
75 ml/5 tbsp stock
450 g/1 lb tomatoes, skinned
2.5 ml/½ tsp dry mustard
Clove garlic, crushed
Salt and pepper

Method

1. Fry the chicken and onion in the oil until brown. Sprinkle over the chilli powder.

2. Add the rest of the ingredients and place in a casserole dish. Bake at 200°C/400°F/gas mark 6 for 45 minutes.

Serves 4 - 6

9 Rabbit Pie

Traditionally a poacher's pie which went out of favour for many years. Rabbit is easily obtainable from most supermarkets and good butchers. With its own distinctive flavour it makes a filling dish for lunch, dinner or supper.

Ingredients

> *1 rabbit*
> *450g/1 lb bacon rashers*
> *15 ml/1 tbsp butter*
> *300ml/½ pt/1¼ cups stock*
> *100 g/4 oz shortcrust pastry*
> *Beaten egg to glaze*

Method

1. Chop the bacon into small pieces and joint the rabbit.

2. Fry the bacon in a frying pan until it is cooked but not brown and add the pieces of rabbit. Cook, turning, until browned on all sides. Place the rabbit and bacon in a deep pie dish. Season with salt and pepper

3. Pour over the stock.

4. Roll out the pastry and cover the pie dish, pressing down the edges to seal in the juices. Pierce a hole in the centre of the pastry and glaze with the beaten egg.

5. Bake at 350°F/180°C/gas mark 4 for 1½ hours.

Serves 4-6

10 Pigeon Casserole

Ingredients

4 pigeons
Salt and freshly ground black pepper
450 ml/¾pt/2 cups dry white wine
2 onions, chopped
2 carrots, chopped
1 bouquet garni
50 g/2 oz/¼ cup butter or margarine
100 g/4 oz belly of pork, rinded and diced
25 g/1 oz/¼ cup plain flour
120 ml/4 fl oz/½ cup brandy
2 cloves garlic, crushed

Method

1. Season the pigeons with salt and pepper. Mix the wine, onions, carrots and bouquet garni, pour over the pigeons, cover and marinate overnight, turning occasionally.

2. Heat three-quarters of the butter or margarine in a flameproof casserole and fry the pork until crisp.

3. Remove the pigeons from the marinade, pat dry on kitchen paper and sprinkle with flour. Add the remaining butter to the casserole and fry the pigeons until browned on all sides. Pour the brandy into the pan and set it alight to burn off the excess fat. Add the strained marinade and the garlic and season with salt and pepper. Cover tightly and cook in a preheated oven at 150°C/300°F/gas mark 2 for 2½ hours. Serve with red cabbage and chestnuts.

Serves 4

11 | Autumn Goose

A goose is generally stuffed with a sage and onion or a prune stuffing. It can be served with blackberry and raisin sauce and is often accompanied by roast apples.

Ingredients

> *1 Goose*
> *100 g/4 oz chopped onion*
> *50 g/2 oz finely chopped sage*
> *100 g/4 oz fresh breadcrumbs*
> *1 egg, beaten*
> *Goose liver, minced*
> *50 g/2 oz/¼ cup butter*

Method

1. Boil the goose liver in a little water for 3-4 minutes. Chop finely and place in a basin.

2. Mix the breadcrumbs into the liver and stir in the onion and chopped sage. Blend in the beaten egg. Stuff this mixture into the goose.

3. Place the bird in a baking tray and prick the skin with a sharp knife. Dot with the butter. Put in the oven at 400°F/200°C/gas mark 6 for 30 minutes. Baste the goose and lower the heat to 350°F/180°C/gas mark 4 for 1½ hours for a 7-8 lb bird.

4. Should the breast of the bird appear to be too brown cover with foil and greaseproof paper for the remainder of the cooking period.

Serves 4- 6

12 Venison with Redcurrant Sauce

Ingredients

4 venison steaks
Few juniper berries, crushed
Salt and freshly ground black pepper
45 ml/3 tbsp olive oil
100 g/4 oz redcurrant jelly
1 stick cinnamon
Juice and shredded rind of 1 lemon
90 ml/6 tbsp port
30 ml/2 tbsp butter, cut into pieces

Method

1. Season the steaks with juniper berries, salt and pepper. Heat the oil and fry the steaks over a high heat until lightly browned on both sides. Reduce the heat and continue to fry until cooked to your liking.

2. Meanwhile, place the redcurrant jelly, cinnamon stick and lemon rind in a pan. Add 30 ml/2 tbsp of port and simmer for 10 minutes. Add the lemon juice then beat in the butter.

3. Transfer the cooked steaks to a warmed serving plate. Add the remaining port to the pan and bring to the boil, stirring to scrape up all the meat juices. Pour over the steaks. Serve the sauce separately.

Serves 4

13 | Edwardian Game

Although this dish was popular at Edwardian tables during the shooting season, it is available for today's market with the produce easily bought from the supermarkets. A rich dish which can be as elaborate or as simple as required.

Ingredients

>   1 pheasant
>   1 partridge
>   2 onions, halved
>   2 carrots, chopped
>   50 g/2 oz/¼ cup butter
>   2 oranges
>   25 g/1 oz/¼ cup flour
>   150 ml/¼ pt/⅔ cup red wine
>   Salt and pepper

Method

1. Place half the butter in a roasting pan and cook the birds in the oven at 350°F/180°C/gas mark 4 for 15 minutes. Remove from the oven and allow to cool.

2. Cut the birds into small joints reserving all skin and odd pieces. Return the joints of the bird to the roasting pan.

3. Place the skin and reserved unwanted pieces of the birds in a large saucepan with 600 ml/1 pint/ 2½ cups water and bring to the boil.

4. Fry the onions and carrots in the remaining butter, stir in the flour and gradually add a little of the strained stock from the skin and odd pieces of the carcass. Stir until the gravy thickens. Season with salt and pepper and pour in the red wine.

5. Grate the rind and remove the juice from the oranges. Stir into the gravy.

6. Pour the sauce over the birds and continue cooking, well covered with greaseproof paper and foil at 300°F/150°C/gas mark 2 for 25 minutes.

Serves 4-6

Beef

Beef makes a wonderful basis for a special-occasion meal; and English cookery has many recipes for the cheaper cuts of beef which are tenderised by long, slow cooking to make delicious and economical family meals.

1 Beef and Ham Roll

Ingredients

450 g/1 lb minced beef
225 g/8 oz minced ham
175 g/6 oz fresh breadcrumbs
15 ml/1 tbsp Worcestershire sauce
Salt and freshly ground black pepper
400 g/14 oz can tomatoes, drained and chopped

Method

1. Mix together the beef, ham, breadcrumbs and Worcestershire sauce and season with salt and pepper. Shape into a roll and place in a greased loaf tin.

2. Bake in a preheated oven at 180°C/350°F/gas mark 4 for 40 minutes.

3. Pour over the tomatoes and bake for a further 15 minutes until the meat is cooked and the tomatoes are hot. Serve with mashed potatoes and a green vegetable.

Serves 4

2 Beef Wellington

Ingredients

1.5 kg/3 lb fillet of beef
Freshly ground black pepper
15 ml/1 tbsp oil
50 g/2 oz/¼ cup butter or margarine
225 g/8 oz button mushrooms, sliced
175 g/6 oz smooth liver pâté
450 g/1 lb puff pastry
1 egg, beaten

Method

1. Trim and tie up the beef and season with pepper. Heat the oil and 15 ml/1 tbsp of the butter or margarine and fry the meat until sealed on all sides.

2. Roast the meat in a preheated oven at 220°C/ 425°F/gas mark 7 for 20 minutes then leave to cool and remove the string.

3. Melt the remaining butter or margarine and fry the mushrooms until soft. Leave to cool then mix with the pâté.

4. Roll out the pastry on a lightly floured surface to a rectangle large enough to enclose the meat completely; trim the edges. Spread the pâté mixture down the centre and place the meat on top. Brush the edges with egg. Fold the pastry up to enclose the meat, sealing the edges with a little egg.

5. Turn the meat over on to a greased baking sheet so that the seams are underneath. Decorate with pastry trimmings and brush well with egg. Bake in a preheated oven at 220°C/425°F/gas mark 7 for 30 minutes then cover with foil and continue to cook for about a further 30 minutes, depending how well done you like your beef.

Serves 8

3 Bubble and Squeak

Ingredients

450 g/1 lb cooked beef
450 g/1 lb cooked cabbage
450 g/1 lb mashed potatoes
75 g/3 oz/⅔ cup butter
Salt and pepper

Method

1. Mince the beef and chop the cooked cabbage. Blend with the mashed potatoes and season well.

2. Heat the butter in a frying pan. Add the beef and cabbage mixture and fry until brown and crispy on both sides. Serve hot.

Serves 4

Steak and Kidney Pie

Ingredients

25 g/1 oz/¼ cup plain flour
Pinch of mustard powder
Pinch of ground mace
Salt and freshly ground black pepper
450 g/1 lb braising steak, cubed
100 g/4 oz ox kidney, cubed
100 g/4 oz mushrooms, chopped
1 onion, chopped
1 clove garlic, crushed
300 ml/½ pt/1¼ cups beef stock
150 ml/¼ pt/⅔ cup port
2.5 ml/½ tsp Worcestershire sauce
1 hard-boiled egg, sliced
For the pastry:
225 g/8 oz/2 cups plain flour
50 g/2 oz/¼ cup butter or margarine
50 g/2 oz/¼ cup lard
30-45 ml/2-3 tbsp water
1 egg, beaten

Method

1. Mix the flour, mustard and mace and season with salt and pepper. Toss the steak and kidney in the seasoned flour then place in a casserole dish with the mushrooms, onion and garlic.

2. Mix the stock, port and Worcestershire sauce and pour over the meat. Cover and cook in a preheated oven at 150°C/300°F/gas mark 2 for 3 hours until the meat is tender. Remove from the oven, chill and skim any fat from the top.

3. Transfer the meat to a pie dish and arrange the egg slices on top.

4. To make the pastry, sift the flour into a bowl with a pinch of salt. Rub in the butter or margarine and lard until the mixture resembles breadcrumbs. Stir in enough water to bind the ingredients to a soft pastry.

5. Roll out the pastry on a lightly floured board. Cut a circle to fit the pie dish and a long strip 2.5 cm/1 in wide and long enough to go round the dish. Moisten the edge of the dish and press the strip all round the dish. Brush with beaten egg and press the lid on top, sealing the edges. Decorate with the pastry trimmings and brush with beaten egg.

6. Bake in a preheated oven at 200°C/400°F/gas mark 6 for about 30 minutes until golden brown.

Serves 4

5 | Roast Beef and Yorkshire Pudding

A traditional Sunday lunch recipe for thousands of English homes. It is a dish known throughout the world and one which every foreign visitor wishes to try at least once. Serve with the characteristic accompaniment of horseradish sauce (see page 137) and a rich brown gravy.

Ingredients

> *Joint of beef*
> *25 g/1 oz/¼ cup flour*
> *Salt*
> *100 g/4 oz/1 cup flour*
> *300ml/½ pt/1¼ cups milk*
> *1 egg*
> *Oil or beef dripping*

Method

1. Heat a little of the oil or beef dripping in a baking tin and brown the meat quickly on all sides to seal in the juices.

2. Pre-heat the oven to 400°F/200°C/gas mark 6. Place the meat in the roasting tin and cook for 20 minutes. Reduce the heat to 350°F/180°C/gas mark 4 for 20 minutes per lb, basting frequently. Remove from the pan and place on a warmed plate. Cover with foil.

3. Heat the oven to 425°F/220°C/gas mark 7. Place the flour into a bowl with the salt and beat in the egg and milk. Allow to stand for 20 minutes. Beat in 1 tablespoon water.

4. Put a tablespoon of the beef dripping in a pudding tin and put in the oven for 5 minutes. Remove from the oven and pour in the batter. Cook for 15-20 minutes until brown and crispy at the edges.

Serves 4

6 Savoury Crumble

Ingredients

450 g/1 lb minced beef
1 onion, chopped
75 ml/5 tbsp stock
175g/6 oz/1½ cups flour
75 g/3 oz/⅔ cup margarine
2.5 ml/½ tsp dry mustard
Salt and pepper

Method

1. Place the mince in a saucepan with the onion and cook, stirring for 5 minutes. Sprinkle over 15ml/1 tbsp flour and pour in the stock. Place in a greased pie dish.

2. Put the flour, mustard, salt and pepper in a bowl and rub in the margarine. Sprinkle over the mince and bake at 200°C/400°F/gas mark 6 for 35 minutes.

Serves 4-6

7 | Beef in Beer

Ingredients

30 ml/2 tbsp oil
450 g/1 lb chuck steak, cubed
100 g/4 oz gammon steak, cubed
2 onions, sliced
1 clove garlic, crushed
300 ml/½ pt/1¼ cups light ale
150 ml/¼ pt/⅔ cup brown ale
5 ml/1 tsp soft brown sugar
5 ml/1 tsp nutmeg
1 bouquet garni
Salt and freshly ground black pepper
5 ml/1 tsp red wine vinegar
15 ml/1 tbsp chopped fresh parsley

Method

1. Heat the oil and fry the steak and gammon until lightly browned on all sides. Lift them from the pan with a slotted spoon and transfer to a casserole dish.

2. Add the onions and garlic to the pan and fry until lightly browned then transfer to the casserole.

3. Add the beers, sugar and nutmeg to the pan, bring to the boil, stirring well to scrape up all the meat juices, then pour into the casserole. Add the bouquet garni and season with salt and pepper. Cover and cook in a preheated oven at 140°C/275°F/gas mark 2 for 3 hours.

4. Remove the bouquet garni, stir in the wine vinegar and serve sprinkled with parsley.

Serves 4

8 Beef Pot Roast

Ingredients

1.75 kg/4 lb brisket of beef, boned and rolled
Salt and freshly ground black pepper
30 ml/2 tbsp lard
1 large onion stuck with 4 cloves
300 ml/½ pt/1¼ cups water
4 carrots, halved lengthways
4 small onions, halved
150 ml/¼ pt/⅔ cup beef stock

Method

1. Tie the meat securely, pat dry with kitchen paper and season with salt and pepper. Heat the lard in a large flameproof casserole and fry the meat until browned on all sides.

2. Add the onion and water, bring to the boil, cover and cook in a preheated oven at 150°C/300°F/gas mark 2 for 2 hours, basting occasionally.

3. Remove the meat, add the carrots and onions then place the meat back on top of them. Cover and return to the oven for a further 1 hour until the meat is tender.

4. Transfer the meat and vegetables to a warmed serving plate and keep them warm. Remove the cloves from the onion. Skim off any excess fat from the cooking liquid, add the stock and bring to the boil, stirring to scrape up all the meat juices from the base of the pan. Strain the sauce into a warmed sauce boat and serve with the beef.

Serves 4

9 Crispy-Topped Mince Pies

Ingredients

100 g/4 oz/½ cup butter or margarine
1 onion, chopped
1 clove garlic, crushed
450 g/1 lb minced beef
100 g/4 oz/1 cup plain flour
300 ml/½ pt/1¼ cups beef stock
2.5 ml/½ tsp thyme
2.5 ml/½ tsp rosemary
2.5 ml/½ tsp nutmeg
Salt and freshly ground black pepper
100 g/4 oz Cheddar cheese, grated

Method

1. Melt 25 g/1 oz/2 tbsp of butter or margarine and fry the onion and garlic until soft. Add the meat and fry until browned. Stir in 15 ml/1 tbsp of flour and cook for 1 minute. Stir in the stock, thyme, rosemary and nutmeg and season with salt and pepper. Simmer, stirring, for 5 minutes then transfer to an ovenproof dish.

2. Rub 50 g/2 oz/¼ cup of butter or margarine into the remaining flour then stir in the cheese. Spread the mixture on top of the mince and dot with the remaining butter or margarine.

3. Bake in a preheated oven at 180°C/350°F/gas mark 4 for 45 minutes until golden brown and crispy.

Serves 4

10 Beef Fillet in Sherry Sauce

Ingredients

4 thin fillet steaks
150 ml/¼ pt/⅔ cup Bristol Cream sherry
15 ml/1 tbsp butter
1 onion, chopped
4 large mushrooms
Dash of Worcestershire sauce
15 ml/1 tbsp chopped parsley
Salt and pepper
60 ml/4 tbsp thick cream

Method

1. Marinate the steaks in the sherry for 3-4 hours. Remove and pat dry.

2. Heat the butter in a frying pan and fry the onion for 2 minutes. Lay in the mushrooms and continue cooking so that they are soft but not crisp.

3. Remove the mushrooms and onion and place in a heated serving dish to keep warm.

4. Heat the pan until very hot then put in the steaks and cook for 3-4 minutes on each side for rare to medium, slightly longer for well-done steaks. Place on top of the mushrooms.

5. Add the sherry marinade, Worcestershire sauce, parsley and season with the salt and pepper. Cook until the liquid is reduced by half. Lower the heat, and stir in the cream. Remove the pan and pour over the steaks. Serve at once.

Serves 4

Lamb and Pork

*Many recipes for lamb and pork
use the slightly sharp flavours of
fruit to balance the richness of
the meat. Others use traditional
herb flavours and slow cooking to
make the meat flavoursome and
succulent.*

North of England Hash

A useful economic recipe for left over cold lamb and a good way of getting children to eat meat. The slightly burnt, crispy edges to the hash give a distinctive flavour to this basic dish. Serve with mushy peas, fried onions and glazed carrots.

Ingredients

450g/1 1b leftover lamb
275 g/10 oz mashed potatoes
50 g/2 oz/¼ cup butter
50 g/2 oz/½ cup flour
15 ml/1 tbsp oil
1 small onion, finely chopped
15 ml/1 tbsp chopped parsley
1 egg

Method

1. Mince the lamb and mix with the potatoes, chopped onion and beaten egg. Blend in the chopped parsley.

2. Form into small cakes using the flour so that the mixture does not stick to the chopping board.

3. Heat the oil and butter in a frying pan, lay in the hash cakes and cook on each side until they are brown. Keep the cakes warm while the rest are cooking.

Serves 4.

2 | Crown Roast of Lamb

Ingredients

1 piece best end of neck of lamb (about 12 chops)
225 g/8 oz pork sausage meat
50 g/2 oz fresh breadcrumbs
50 g/2 oz mushrooms, chopped
10 ml/2 tsp lemon juice
10 ml/2 tsp made mustard
Salt and freshly ground black pepper
4 tomatoes, halved
15 ml/1 tbsp chopped fresh rosemary
50 g/2 oz/¼ cup butter or margarine
1 clove garlic, crushed

Method

1. Trim the meat and cut off and discard the top 2.5 cm/1 in of fat to expose the bones. Trim the meat between the bones and chop it finely. Shape the meat into a circle and tie securely. Arrange in a roasting tin and score the fat on the outside.

2. Mix the chopped meat with the sausage meat, breadcrumbs, mushrooms, half the lemon juice and half the mustard. Season with salt and pepper. Scoop out the centres of the tomatoes and add to the mixture. Press most of the mixture gently into the centre of the roast and the rest into the tomato shells.

3. Mix together the remaining lemon juice and mustard with the rosemary, butter or margarine and garlic and rub over the outside of the meat.

4. Bake in a preheated oven at 190°C/350°F/gas mark 5 for 45 minutes. Arrange the tomatoes around the meat and bake for a further 45 minutes or until the lamb is cooked.

Serves 4-6

3 Roast Lamb with Nut and Apricot Stuffing

Ingredients

1 onion, finely chopped
150 g/5 oz breadcrumbs
100 g/4 oz dried no-need-to-soak apricots, chopped
100 g/4 oz/1 cup chestnuts, chopped
1 egg, beaten
Salt and freshly ground black pepper
1 boned shoulder of lamb

Method

1. Mix together the onion, breadcrumbs, apricots, chestnuts and egg and season with salt and pepper.

2. Lay the lamb joint flat and cover with the stuffing. Roll up the meat over the stuffing and tie securely with string.

3. Place the lamb on a rack in a roasting tin filled with a little water. Roast in a preheated oven at 400°C/200°F/gas mark 6 for 15 minutes then reduce the heat to 180°C/350°F/gas mark 4 and continue to cook for a further 2 hours or until the lamb is tender. Add a little more water to the pan during cooking, if necessary, and baste occasionally with the meat juices.

Serves 6

4 | Liver and Bacon

Ingredients

15 ml/1 tbsp oil
4 onions, sliced
450 g/1 lb lambs' liver, sliced
15 ml/1 tbsp plain flour
300 ml/½ pt/1¼ cups beef stock
Salt and freshly ground black pepper
8 rashers streaky bacon

Method

1. Heat the oil and fry the onions until lightly browned. Add the liver and fry gently until just browned on both sides.

2. Stir in the flour and cook for 1 minute. Stir in the stock and bring to the boil, stirring. Simmer, stirring continuously, until the gravy thickens. Cover and simmer for 10 minutes until the liver is tender. Season to taste with salt and pepper.

3. Meanwhile, grill the bacon rashers until crisp and browned.

4. Transfer the liver and gravy to a warmed serving dish, surround with the crisp bacon and serve at once.

Serves 4

5 | Bacon Roly Poly

A tasty old fashioned recipe very filling for cold day dinners. Serve with cabbage and boiled, new potatoes.

Ingredients

225g/8 oz/2 cups self-raising flour
225g/8 oz lean bacon, chopped
75g/3 oz suet
Salt and pepper
3 large onions, chopped
10 ml/2 tsps fresh sage, chopped
5 ml/1 tsp nutmeg

Method

1. Mix the flour, suet, salt and pepper with enough water to form a light dough. Roll out on a floured board to form a rectangular shape.

2. Lay the chopped onion and bacon over the dough. Sprinkle with the sage and nutmeg. Roll up gently.

3. Wrap in a well-floured cloth and lay in a large saucepan. Pour water over the roly poly and boil for 2½ hours topping up with water whenever necessary.

4. Unwrap the roll and serve in thick slices with a white sauce (see page 140).

Serves 4

6 Devilled Kidneys

Served at the Reform Club in London for many years and eaten in Edwardian times at breakfast, this spicy dish makes a superb supper if served with rice.

Ingredients

> 3 sheep's kidneys
> 30 ml/2 tbsp port or sherry
> 30 ml/2 tbsp butter
> 2½ ml/½ tsp freshly chopped sage
> 1 tbsp flour

Method

1. Skin the kidneys and cut into small pieces.

2. Heat the butter in a frying pan and fry the kidneys for 3-4 minutes. Stir in the port and sprinkle with the flour and chopped sage. Stir well and cook for a further minute.

3. Pour into two individual dishes and keep hot. Garnish with parsley if desired.

Serves 2

7 | Honey Roast Ham

The sweet honey crust on the ham, previously studded
with cloves gives a seasonal aroma to any kitchen. Use cold,
in summer or hot in winter and serve with freshly cooked
new potatoes and pickles or mustard.

Ingredients

1 joint of ham approximately 1.25 kg/2½ lb
8 cloves
60 ml/4 tbsp honey
30 ml/2 tbsp butter
75 g/3 oz/⅓ cup demerara sugar
White wine or cider

Method

1. Soak the ham overnight in cold water to extract the
   salt. Dry and place in a baking tray with the butter.

2. Score the fat into diamond shaped patterns and
   bake at 375°F/190°C/gas mark 5 for 25 minutes
   per 450 g/1 1b, basting occasionally.

3. 1 hour before the cooking is finished stud the rind
   with the cloves and pour over the honey, wine and
   demerara sugar. Continue cooking, basting every
   10 minutes.

Serves 4-6

8 | Sausage and Apple Yorkshires

Ingredients

225 g/8 oz pork sausage meat
2 cooking apples, peeled, cored and grated
5 ml/1 tsp chopped fresh parsley
salt and freshly ground black pepper
100 g/4 oz/1 cup plain flour
2 eggs, lightly beaten
300 ml/½ pt/⅔ cup milk

Method

1. Mix together the sausage meat, apples and parsley and season with salt and pepper. Shape into small balls and arrange in 4 greased individual ovenproof dishes.

2. Bake in a preheated oven at 220°C/425°F/gas mark 7 for 10 minutes.

3. Meanwhile, beat together the flour, eggs and milk and season with a little salt. Pour into the dishes and return to the oven for 35 minutes until well risen and golden brown. Serve with gravy.

Serves 4

9 Pork with Apple and Honey

Ingredients

225 g/8 oz haricot beans
450 g/1 lb lean belly of pork
15 ml/1 tbsp clear honey
600 ml/1 pt/2½ cups chicken stock
300 ml/½ pt/1¼ cups apple juice
4 cloves
1 onion
1 bouquet garni
3 carrots, sliced
2 leeks, sliced
2 stalks celery, sliced
30 ml/2 tbsp Worcestershire sauce
15 ml/1 tbsp tomato purée
Salt and freshly ground black pepper

Method

1. Soak the beans overnight in cold water then drain. Rind the pork and cut it into chunks.

2. Place the pork in a flameproof casserole over a medium heat until the fat begins to run. Add the beans, honey, stock and apple juice. Press the cloves into the onion and add it to the pan with the bouquet garni. Bring to the boil, cover and simmer for 1 hour until the beans are just tender.

3.   Add the remaining ingredients and season with salt and pepper. Return to the boil and simmer, uncovered, for a further 20 minutes until the vegetables are tender and the liquid has reduced slightly. Discard the bouquet garni and serve with jacket potatoes or crusty bread.

Serves 4

10 Bean and Bacon Hot Pot

Ingredients

100 g/4 oz haricot beans
225 g/8 oz bacon pieces, chopped
5 ml/1 tsp chopped fresh herbs
2 onions, finely chopped
3 carrots, chopped
3 tomatoes, chopped
300 ml/½ pint/1¼ cups stock
Salt and pepper

Method

1.   Soak the beans in cold water ovemight. Next day, bring to the boil in a casserole dish. Add the bacon, vegetables, stock and herbs. Season. Place in the oven and cook at 180°C/350°F/gas mark 4 for 1 hour.

Serves 3-4

11 | Pork and Chicken Layer Pie

Ingredients

275 g/10 oz/2½ cups plain flour
Salt
50 g/2 oz/¼ cup lard
75 g/3 oz/⅓ cup butter or margarine
2 eggs, beaten
350 g/12 oz lean pork, finely chopped
1 onion, finely chopped
100 g/4 oz belly of pork, rinded and finely chopped
5 ml/1 tsp marjoram
Freshly ground black pepper
100 g/4 oz cooked chicken, cut into strips

Method

1. Mix the flour and a pinch of salt then rub in the lard and butter or margarine until the mixture resembles breadcrumbs. Reserve half an egg for glazing and mix to a firm pastry with the remainder. Cover and chill until required.

2. Mix the pork, onion, belly pork and marjoram and season with salt and pepper. Cut a 2.5 cm/1 in double strip of greaseproof paper and lay it along the length of a 450 g/1 lb loaf tin, sticking out at each end.

3. Divide the pastry into six and roll it out into rectangles to fit the sides, base and top of the tin. Seal the base and sides together by damping them with water and pressing them together. Fill the tin with half the pork mixture, lay the chicken on top, then add the remaining pork. Seal on the lid, pinching round the edge to seal and make a pattern. Roll out any trimmings and decorate the top of the pie with pastry leaves. Glaze well with beaten egg and cut 3 steam vents in the top.

4. Bake in a preheated oven at 200°C/400°F/gas mark 6 for 45 minutes then reduce the temperature to 160°C/325°F/gas mark 3 for a further 45 minutes. Leave to cool in the tin.

Serves 4

12 Lamb and Beans

A farmhouse standby, this recipe is cheap to produce with very little effort and is nourishing as well as tasty. Serve with mustard and a green vegetable.

Ingredients

4 lamb chops
450 g/1 lb butter beans
675 g/1½ lb potatoes
600 ml/1 pt chicken stock
1 onion, sliced
Salt and Pepper

Method

1. Soak the beans for 24 hours in cold water, then drain.

2. Peel and slice the potatoes and lay in the bottom of a pie-dish. Lay over the butter beans. Sprinkle over the sliced onions and season with the salt and pepper.

3. Place the lamb chops on the top and season again. Pour over the stock and cover tightly with a lid or foil. Bake in the oven at 350°F/180°C/gas mark 4 for 2 hours.

Serves 4

13 Smoked Bacon Rolls

These delicious bacon rolls can be served with drinks or as an accompaniment to a main meal on little squares of fried bread or toast.

Ingredients

8 back bacon rashers
175 g/6 oz/1½ cups cheese, grated
5 ml/1 tsp milk
30 ml/2 tbsp cream
5 ml/1 tsp ready-made mustard
10 ml/2 tsp Worcestershire sauce
5 ml/1 tsp freshly chopped sage

Method

1. Put the cheese in a bowl and blend in the milk, cream, mustard, Worcestershire sauce and sage.

2. When the mixture is thoroughly blended divide equally between the rashers. Roll up, starting at the wide end and secure with a cocktail stick.

3. Lay the bacon rolls on a heated grill and cook for 5-6 minutes turning frquently.

Makes 8

Eggs and Cheese

*Popular for light meals, snacks
and lunches, egg and cheese
dishes can be served with salads
or vegetables to make a
substantial and appetising meal.*

1 Welsh Rarebit

Ingredients

50 g/2 oz/¼ cup butter or margarine
175 g/6 oz Cheddar cheese, grated
5 ml/1 tsp made mustard
15 ml/1 tbsp single cream
Pinch of cayenne pepper
Salt and freshly ground black pepper
1 egg, beaten
4 slices bread

Method

1. Melt half the butter or margarine in a pan. Stir in the cheese, mustard and cream and season with cayenne pepper, salt and pepper. Continue to stir over a low heat until the mixture is smooth. Remove from the heat and beat in the egg.

2. Toast the bread and spread with the remaining butter. Spread the cheese mixture over the toast and grill until golden brown. Serve at once.

Serves 4

2 Baked Vegetables with Cheese

Ingredients

1 aubergine, peeled and sliced
Salt and freshly ground black pepper
25 g/1 oz/¼ cup plain flour
150 ml/¼ pt/⅔ cup oil
2 onions, chopped
3 tomatoes, skinned and chopped
2 cloves garlic, crushed
2.5 ml/½ tsp dried basil
30 ml/2 tbsp chopped fresh parsley
60 ml/4 tbsp cream sherry
350 g/12 oz cheese, grated

Method

1. Sprinkle the aubergine generously with salt and leave to stand for 30 minutes. Rinse in cold water, drain and pat dry. Season the flour with salt and pepper and coat the aubergine in the flour.

2. Heat the oil and fry the aubergine until lightly browned on both sides. Remove from the pan and drain on kitchen paper. Add the onions, tomatoes, garlic and herbs to the pan and simmer, stirring frequently, until the vegetables are cooked and mushy. Season with salt and pepper and stir in the sherry.

3. Pour one-third of the sauce into a greased ovenproof dish, arrange half the aubergine on top and sprinkle with one-third of the cheese. Repeat the layers of sauce, aubergine slices and cheese, then top with the remaining sauce, reserving the remaining cheese.

4. Bake in a preheated oven at 190°C/375°F/gas mark 5 for 35 minutes until the aubergine slices are soft when pierced with a skewer. Sprinkle with the remaining cheese and return to the oven until the cheese melts and browns. Serve at once.

Serves 4

3 | Soldiers Sandwich

A snack dating from before the first world war and often served to use up leftover cheese.

Ingredients

50 g/2 oz/¼ cup butter
2.5 ml/½ tsp ready-made mustard
100 g/4 oz grated cheese
8 thick slices of bread
1 egg
Salt and pepper

Method

1. Beat half the butter with the mustard and egg. Stir in the grated cheese, salt and pepper.

2. Put a thick layer of the cheese mixture between two slices of bread and fill the rest of the sandwiches in the same way.

3. Melt the remaining butter in a frying pan and fry the sandwiches until the filling begins to melt and both sides of the bread are crisp and brown.

Serves 4

4 | Sweet Omelettes

Very popular in Edwardian times and almost ignored today, sweet omelettes are quick and easy to prepare and serve. The addition of fresh fruit gives that sharply, sweet flavour to finish a meal with a touch of flourish.

Ingredients

2 egg yolks
3 egg whites
75 g/3 oz raspberries cleaned and hulled
30 ml/2 tbsp butter
25 g/1 oz caster sugar
Fresh cream if desired

Method

1. Beat the sugar and the egg yolks together until the yolks are lighter in colour.

2. Whisk the egg whites until stiff and stir them lightly into the egg yolks.

3. Melt the butter in a shallow frying pan and when smoking hot pour in the batter.

4. Allow to cook for 2 minutes. Place the raspberries on one half of the omelette. Fold over the other half of the batter and cook for 1 minute. Slide on to a dish and serve at once sprinkled with extra sugar and cream if desired.

Makes 2

5 Deep Fried Cheese Balls

Once a delicate savoury for after dinner parties these spicy cheese balls can be served with drinks or at festive occasions as well as picnics.

Ingredients

30 ml/2 tbsp butter
100 ml/3½ fl oz water
100 g/4 oz/½ cup flour
1 tsp cayenne pepper
2.5 ml/½ tsp nutmeg
75 g/3 oz Cheddar cheese, grated
3 egg yolks
2 egg whites
Salt and pepper
Oil for frying

Method

1. Put the butter and water into a saucepan and bring to the boil. Shake the flour over the water and reduce the heat. Stir briskly for 1 minute until the batter is thick.

2. Remove from the heat and beat in the egg yolks, one at a time. Stir in the cheese, nutmeg, cayenne pepper, salt and pepper.

3. Whisk the egg whites and fold into the mixture.

4.   Heat the oil to boiling and drop tiny spoonfuls of the mixture into the hot fat. Fry until golden brown. Remove and dry on kitchen paper. For extra flavour Parmesan cheese can be sprinkled over the cheese balls.

Makes 36

6 | Cheese Tarts

Ingredients

> 100 g/4 oz cream cheese
> 75g/3 oz/⅓ cup sugar
> Pinch nutmeg
> 350 g/12 oz shortcrust pastry
> Grated rind and juice of 1 lemon
> 3 egg yolks

Method

1.   Line greased tartlet tins with the rolled out pastry.

2.   Blend the cream cheese, sugar, egg yolks, nutmeg and lemon juice and rind together. Pour the mixture into the pastry cases and bake at 200°C/400°F/gas mark 6 for 25 minutes.

Serves 6

7 | Cheese Pasties

A traditional recipe throughout many counties of England, each having its own variation. An extremely useful addition to a summer picnic this recipe can also be served hot for a supper dish. The stronger the flavour of the cheese used the more characteristic the pasty becomes.

Ingredients

> 450 g/1 lb shortcrust pastry
> 350 g/12 oz Cheshire or Stilton, coarsely grated
> 100 g/4 oz/½ cup butter
> 1 egg, beaten
> 2.5 ml/½ tsp cayenne pepper
> 5 ml/1 tsp nutmeg
> Salt and pepper
> 1 small onion, finely chopped

Method

1. Roll out the pastry and cut into rounds the size of a small saucer.

2. Mix the crumbled or grated cheese with the butter, cayenne, nutmeg and chopped onion.

3. Put a tablespoon of the mixture into the centre of each round of pastry. Season with salt and pepper. Moisten the edges of the pastry with the egg and fold over.

4. Press the edges of the pastry with a fork to make a patterned edge. Brush the top of the pasty with beaten egg and bake at 400°F/200°C/gas mark 6 for 15-20 minutes.

Makes 10-12 pasties

8 | Cheese Straws

Once served as an after dinner savoury to eat with cheese, these straws have found their way into children's parties, barbecues and picnics. Any type of cheese or leftover pieces can be used for this recipe. They are particularly pleasant at Christmastime when the rich fare of most cook's tables lays heavy on the stomach and the waistline. Cheese straws can be served hot or cold and re-heat perfectly. They are ideal for keeping in the freezer.

Ingredients

175 g/6 oz puff pastry
100 g/4 oz grated cheese
15 ml/1 tbsp flour
2.5 ml/½ tsp cayenne pepper
Salt and pepper
1 egg, beaten

Method

1. Roll the pastry out thinly and sprinkle over with the grated cheese, cayenne and salt and pepper. Fold in half and roll out once again, towards the fold, to seal in the cheese and spices. Fold and roll again.

2. Cut into thin stips and glaze with the beaten egg. Bake on a lightly floured baking tin at 425°F/220°C/gas mark 7 for 6-8 minutes.

Makes 35

Vegetables and Pulses

Whether you want interesting vegetable dishes to accompany a meat course, or vegetables which can be served as a meal in themselves, take advantage of the excellent variety of vegetables available in the supermarket to make some delicious dishes.

1 Baked Beetroot with Soured Cream

Ingredients

4 beetroots
150 ml/¼ pt/⅔ cup soured cream
Salt and freshly ground black pepper

Method

1. Clean the beetroots but do not trim them. Wrap in greased foil and place in a greased ovenproof dish. Cover and bake in a preheated oven at 180°C/350°F/gas mark 4 for 2½ hours until tender.

2. Unwrap the beetroots, trim them and slide off the skin. Arrange on a warmed serving plate and top with a spoonful of soured cream. Season to taste with salt and pepper and serve at once.

Serves 4

2 | Broccoli in Lemon Sauce

Ingredients

450 g/1 lb broccoli florets
Salt
Grated rind and juice of 1 lemon
5 ml/1 tsp sugar
30 ml/2 tbsp cornflour
30 ml/2 tbsp water
15 ml/1 tbsp flaked almonds, toasted

Method

1. Cook the broccoli in boiling salted water for 10 minutes then drain and reserve 300 ml/½ pt/ 1¼ cups of the cooking liquid. Transfer the broccoli to a warmed serving dish and keep it warm while making the sauce.

2. Add the lemon rind, juice and sugar to the measured cooking liquid and season to taste with salt. Mix the cornflour and water to a paste then stir it into the liquid. Bring to the boil, stirring continuously, then simmer until the sauce becomes thick and clear.

3. Pour the sauce over the broccoli and serve garnished with almonds.

Serves 4

3 Carrots with Mint and Lemon

Ingredients

450 g/1 lb carrots, sliced
Salt and freshly ground black pepper
Grated rind and juice of 1 lemon
15 ml/1 tbsp soft brown sugar
15 ml/1 tbsp butter or margarine
30 ml/2 tbsp chopped fresh mint

Method

1. Cook the carrots in boiling water for about 15 minutes until tender. Drain and return to the hot pan.

2. Add the remaining ingredients, cover, and shake the pan or stir gently until the butter is melted and the carrots are well coated in the sauce. Serve at once.

Serves 4

4 Celery Bake

Ingredients

1 head celery, cut into chunks
2.5 ml/½ tsp ground allspice
2 cloves garlic, crushed
300 ml/½ pt/1¼ cups single cream
Salt and freshly ground black pepper
45 ml/3 tbsp fresh wholemeal breadcrumbs
45 ml/3 tbsp grated cheese

Method

1. Arrange the celery chunks in a greased ovenproof dish.

2. Mix together the spice, garlic and cream and season with salt and pepper. Pour over the celery. Mix together the breadcrumbs and cheese and sprinkle over the top.

3. Bake in a preheated oven at 200°C/400°F/gas mark 6 for about 1 hour or until the celery is tender. Serve hot.

Serves 4

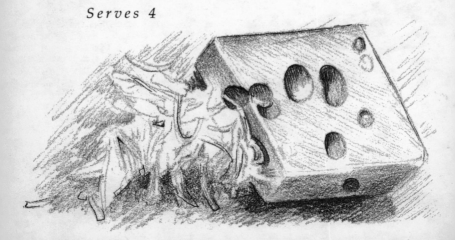

5 Stuffed Courgettes

Ingredients

6 courgettes
50 g/2 oz/¼ cup butter or margarine
1 onion, chopped
1 clove garlic, crushed
2.5 ml/½ tsp paprika
30 ml/2 tbsp tomato purée
4 tomatoes, skinned and chopped
2.5 ml/½ tsp dried oregano
2.5 ml/½ tsp dried basil
175 g/6 oz cooked long-grain rice
100 g/4 oz strong Cheddar cheese, grated

Method

1. Trim the stalks and boil the courgettes, whole and unpeeled, for 5 minutes. Drain, rinse in cold water and cut in half lengthways. Scoop out the seeds and flesh to make boat shapes, reserving the flesh.

2. Melt the butter or margarine and fry the onion and garlic until soft but not browned. Add the courgette flesh and all the other ingredients except the cheese and simmer gently, stirring frequently, for 5 minutes.

3. Pile the stuffing into the courgette boats and arrange in a greased ovenproof dish. Sprinkle with the cheese and bake in a preheated oven at 190°C/375°F/gas mark 5 for 20 minutes until crispy and golden brown on top.

Serves 4-6

6 Leek and Bacon Toastie

Ingredients

50 g/2 oz/¼ cup butter or margarine
4 leeks, sliced
Salt and freshly ground black pepper
100 g/4 oz strong cheese, grated
4 slices bread
8 rashers streaky bacon

Method

1. Melt the butter or margarine and fry the leeks until soft.

2. Season to taste with salt and pepper and stir in the cheese. Cover and simmer very gently until the leeks are tender.

3. Toast the bread and grill the bacon until crisp. Arrange the toast on a warmed serving plate, spoon over the leeks and top with the bacon. Serve at once.

Serves 4

7 Pan Haggerty

Ingredients

25 g/1 oz butter or margarine
15 ml/1 tbsp oil
450 g/1 lb potatoes, thinly sliced
2 onions, thinly sliced
100 g/4 oz Cheddar or Lancashire cheese, grated
Salt and freshly ground black pepper

Method

1. Heat the butter and oil in a heavy-based frying pan. Remove the pan from the heat and add layers of potatoes, onions and cheese, seasoning with salt and pepper as you add each layer. Finish with a layer of potatoes and then cheese.

2. Return to a gentle heat, cover and cook for about 30 minutes until the potatoes and onions are just cooked.

3. Remove the lid and brown the cheese under a hot grill before serving.

Serves 4

8 | Vegetable Hot Pot

Ingredients

30 ml/2 tbsp oil
30 ml/2 tbsp butter or margarine
2 onions, sliced
1 clove garlic, crushed
1 leek, sliced
2 carrots, cubed
2 potatoes, cubed
30 ml/2 tbsp tomato purée
25 g/1 oz/¼ cup plain flour
250 ml/8 fl oz/1 cup dry red wine
300 ml/½ pt/1¼ cups vegetable stock
5 ml/1 tsp dried marjoram
5 ml/1 tsp dried thyme
225 g/8 oz button mushrooms
150 ml/¼ pt/⅔ cup single cream
100 g/4 oz blue cheese, crumbled
Salt and freshly ground black pepper
15 ml/1 tbsp chopped fresh parsley

Method

1. Heat the oil and butter or margarine and fry the onions, garlic and leek until soft but not browned. Add the carrots and potatoes and fry until very lightly browned.

2. Stir in the tomato purée. Stir in the flour and cook for 1 minute. Stir in the wine, stock, marjoram, thyme and mushrooms, bring to the boil, cover and simmer for 30 minutes.

3. If the sauce is a little thin, remove the lid and simmer until reduced slightly. Alternatively, mix 15 ml/1 tbsp cornflour to a paste with a little water, stir into the pan and simmer, stirring, until the sauce thickens.

4. Stir in the cream and cheese and season to taste with salt and pepper. Serve sprinkled with parsley.

Serves 4

9 Cinnamon Carrots

Ingredients

450g/1 lb carrots, coarsely grated
10 ml/2 tsp ground cinnamon
Salt and pepper
30 ml/2 tbsp butter, melted

Method

1. Place the grated carrots in an oven dish with the salt and pepper, cinnamon and melted butter. Cover with foil and bake for 1 hour at 180°C/350°F/gas mark 4.

Serves 4

10 Lentil Stew with Dumplings

Ingredients

225 g/8 oz lentils, soaked
600 ml/1 pt/2½ cups vegetable stock
225 g/8 oz baby carrots
100 g/4 oz mushrooms, sliced
2 large onions, finely chopped
30 ml/2 tbsp vinegar
2.5 ml/½ tsp thyme
Salt and freshly ground black pepper
100 g/4 oz/1 cup self-raising flour
50 g/2 oz shredded suet
½ small onion, finely chopped
15 ml/1 tbsp chopped fresh parsley
30 ml/2 tbsp water

Method

1. Drain the lentils and place in a large saucepan with the stock, carrots, mushrooms, large onions, vinegar and thyme. Season with salt and pepper, bring to the boil, cover and simmer for 30 minutes until the lentils are tender.

2. Continue cooking, stirring frequently, until the lentils go mushy, adding a little more stock or water if necessary.

3. Make the dumplings by mixing all the remaining ingredients, adding enough water to make a firm dough. Roll the mixture into small dumplings and cook separately in boiling stock or water for about 30 minutes then add to the stew and serve.

Serves 4

11 Baked Onions

Onions add flavour to so many dishes that we often forget they can be used on their own as a versatile vegetable. Try them this way when cooking a baked dish such as Lamb and Beans (see page 80). The aromatic smell of baked onions when they come out of the oven complements the dish. My grandmother used to serve onions in this way if any of the family had a heavy cold or a sore throat, as it was said that baked onions, served with lashings of butter, were a certain cure for this ailment!

Ingredients

> 4 large onions, allowing one for each serving
> 100 ml/3½ fl oz/¼ cup stock
> 30 ml/2 tbsp butter

Method

1. Butter a pie dish. Leave the onions in their skins but be sure they are clean. Place side by side in the pie dish and pour the stock around the base of the onions.

2. Bake at 375°F/190°C/gas mark 5 for 1½ to 2 hours. Peel off the outer skins carefully as they will be very hot, and serve whole sprinkled with salt and pepper.

Serves 4

12 | Creamed Parsnips

The taste of parsnips was used during the last war as a sweetener to many dishes both for desserts and savouries. They are not used today as often as they might be and when they are the recipe is normally for baked parsnips. Try this way of cooking them for a supper dish and serve with baked gammon or poultry.

Ingredients

450 g/1 lb parsnips
30 ml/2 tbsp butter
30 ml/2 tbsp thick cream
75 g/3 oz grated cheese
3 tbsp fresh breadcrumbs
2.5 ml/¼ tsp ready made mustard
2.5 ml/¼ tsp nutmeg
Salt and pepper

Method

1. Peel the parsnips and boil in salted water until tender, approximately 20 minutes.

2. Mash or blend them until soft. Mix in the nutmeg, mustard and half the butter. Season with the salt and pepper.

3. Butter a pie dish and layer half the parsnip mixture into the bottom. Sprinkle over half the grated cheese and season again. Lay over the remaining parsnips.

4. Mix the breadcrumbs and remaining cheese together and add to the dish. Dot any remaining butter over the top of the breadcrumbs and bake in the oven at 375°F/190°C/gas mark 5 for 20-25 minutes until golden on top.

Serves 4.

13 Turnips in Cheese Sauce

Although many people do not like the strong flavour of turnips, once cooked in this way they make a deliciously different vegetable accompaniment to many baked dishes.

Ingredients

12 young turnips
75 g/3 oz/⅔ cups butter
25 g/1 oz/¼ cup flour
75 g/3 oz grated cheese
3 tbsp fresh breadcrumbs
300 ml/½ pt/1¼ cups milk
2.5 ml/¼ tsp nutmeg

Method

1. Peel the turnips and leave whole. Boil in salted water for 20 minutes until tender. Drain and allow to cool a little. Cut them into slices.

2. Butter a pie dish and lay in the slices, evenly.

3. Heat half the remaining butter in a saucepan. Blend in the flour and gradually stir in the milk. Cook until thickened and mix in the cheese. Pour over the turnips.

4. Mix the nutmeg, breadcrumbs and salt and pepper together and lay over the turnips and cheese sauce. Dot with any remaining butter and bake at 375°F/190°C/gas mark 5 for 20-25 minutes until brown and crispy. Serve at once.

Serves 4

Desserts

*The English are excellent at
making wonderful desserts to
round off any meal – whether a
simple family meal in the height
of winter or a sophisticated
summer dinner party with
friends.*

Bakewell Tart

Ingredients

100 g/4 oz/1 cup plain flour
100 g/4 oz/½ cup margarine
45 ml/3 tbsp water
100 g/4 oz raspberry jam
50 g/2 oz/¼ cup caster sugar
1 egg, lightly beaten
2.5 ml/½ tsp almond essence
25 g/1 oz/¼ cup self-raising flour
25 g/1 oz ground almonds

Method

1. Sift the flour into a bowl. Rub in half the margarine until the mixture resembles fine breadcrumbs. Add just enough water to mix to a soft pastry.

2. Roll out the pastry on a lightly floured surface and use to line a greased 18 cm/7 in flan ring. Spread the pastry with jam.

3. Cream the remaining margarine with the sugar until light and fluffy. Beat in the egg and almond essence then stir in the flour and ground almonds. Spread over the jam, sealing the edges to the pastry.

4. Bake in a preheated oven at 190°C/350°F/gas mark 4 for 20 minutes. Leave to cool slightly then cut into fingers.

Serves 4

2 Bread and Butter Pudding

Ingredients

8 slices stale wholemeal bread
50 g/2 oz/¼ cup butter or margarine
100 g/4 oz sultanas
75 g/3 oz/1⅓ cup soft brown sugar
2 eggs, lightly beaten
600 ml/1 pt/2½ cups milk
5 ml/1 tsp mixed spice
30 ml/2 tbsp demerara sugar

Method

1. Spread the bread with the butter or margarine and cut each slice into 4 triangles. Layer the bread in a greased ovenproof dish, sprinkling each layer with sultanas and sugar. Finish with bread slices.

2. Stir the eggs into the milk with the mixed spice and pour slowly over the pudding. Leave to stand for at least 30 minutes. Sprinkle with demerara sugar.

3. Bake in a preheated oven at 180°C/350°F/gas mark 4 for about 45 minutes until the top is crisp and golden and the inside fluffy.

Serves 4

3 Coffee Fudge Pudding

Ingredients

100 g/4 oz/½ cup butter or margarine
175 g/6 oz/¾ cup soft brown sugar
1 egg, beaten
45 ml/3 tbsp strong black coffee
100 g/4 oz/1 cup plain flour
25 g/1 oz/¼ cup chopped mixed nuts
300 ml/½ pt/1¼ cups milk

Method

1. Beat the butter or margarine with 100 g/4 oz/ ½ cup of sugar until soft. Beat in the egg, coffee, flour and nuts, adding a little milk to make a soft mixture. Spoon into a greased ovenproof dish.

2. Mix together the remaining sugar and milk and pour over the pudding.

3. Bake in a preheated oven at 160°C/325°F/gas mark 3 for 1½ hours until spongy to the touch. The pudding has a light sponge topping and a coffee sauce underneath.

Serves 4

Spotted Dick with Rum Sauce

Ingredients

175 g/6 oz/1½ cups plain flour
Pinch of salt
75 g/3 oz shredded suet
50 g/2 oz/¼ cup caster sugar
1 egg, lightly beaten
90 ml/6 tbsp milk
175 g/6 oz dates, chopped
For the sauce:
30 ml/2 tbsp butter
30 ml/2 tbsp plain flour
300 ml/½ pt/1¼ cups milk
15 ml/1 tbsp sugar
45 ml/3 tbsp rum

Method

1. Mix together the flour, salt, suet and sugar. Make a well in the centre and stir in the egg and enough milk to give a soft consistency. Stir in the dates.

2. Turn the mixture into a greased pudding basin, cover with pleated greaseproof paper and foil or a cloth and tie with string. Stand in a pan filled with water to come half way up the sides of the basin, cover and steam for about 2 hours until well risen.

3.   To make the sauce, melt the butter, stir in the flour and cook over a low heat, stirring, for 1 minute, without letting the flour brown. Remove from the pan and add the milk. Return to the heat and bring to the boil, stirring, then simmer until the sauce thickens. Stir in the sugar and rum to taste.

Serves 4

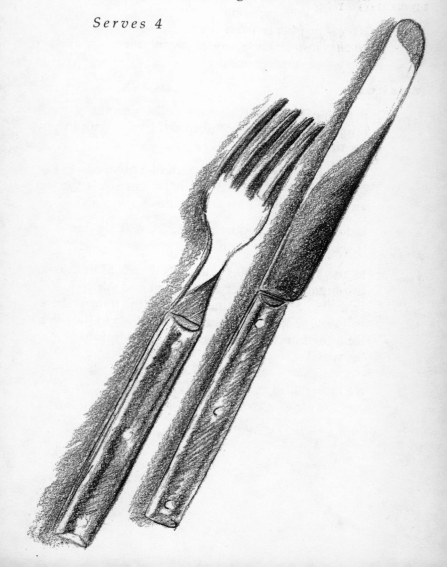

5 | Queen of Puddings

Ingredients

4 eggs
600 ml/1 pt/2½ cups milk
100 g/4 oz fresh breadcrumbs
75 ml/5 tbsp strawberry or raspberry jam
100 g/4 oz/½ cup caster sugar

Method

1. Separate 3 eggs and beat the yolks with the remaining whole egg. Stir into the milk with the breadcrumbs.

2. Spoon the jam over the bottom of a greased ovenproof dish. Pour the milk mixture over the top and leave to stand for 40 minutes.

3. Bake in a preheated oven at 150°C/300°F/gas mark 2 for 1 hour until set.

4. Whisk the egg whites until stiff then fold in most of the sugar. Spoon over the custard and sprinkle with the remaining sugar. Reduce the temperature to 140°C/275°F/gas mark 1 and return to the oven for a further 25 minutes until set and lightly browned.

Serves 4

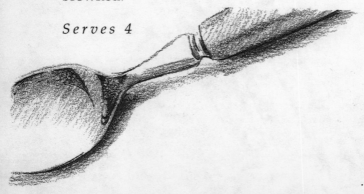

6 | Cider Syllabub

Ingredients

1 orange
150 ml/¼ pt/⅔ cup medium cider
60 ml/4 tbsp caster sugar
300 ml/½ pt/1¼ cups double cream

Method

1. Pare off a few strips of orange rind and cut into very thin shreds. Blanch in boiling water for 3 minutes then drain well. Grate the remaining rind finely then place in a bowl with 60 ml/4 tbsp of orange juice, the cider and sugar. Stir until the sugar dissolves then leave to stand for 2 hours.

2. Whip the cream until just stiff then whisk in the cider just until the syllabub thickens. It may curdle if you overbeat the mixture. Spoon into tall glasses, garnish with the orange shreds and chill before serving.

Serves 4

7 Gooseberry Fool

Ingredients

450 g/1 lb gooseberries, trimmed
30 ml/2 tbsp water
45 ml/3 tbsp clear honey
75 g/3 oz/⅓ cup sugar
300 ml/½ pt/1¼ cups double cream

Method

1. Place the gooseberries in a pan with the water and simmer over a gentle heat, stirring frequently, until soft. Purée or rub through a sieve. Stir in the honey and sugar and leave to cool.

2. Whip the cream until just stiff then fold it into the gooseberries and chill before serving.

Serves 4

8 English Trifle

Ingredients

600 ml/1 pt/2½ cups milk
1 vanilla pod
2 eggs
2 egg yolks
30 ml/2 tbsp caster sugar
10 trifle sponges or stale cake
175 g/6 oz jam
100 g/4 oz macaroons, crumbled
90 ml/6 tbsp sweet sherry
300 ml/½ pt/1¼ cups double cream
30 ml/2 tbsp flaked almonds, toasted

Method

1. Bring the milk almost to the boil with the vanilla pod. Leave to cool for 20 minutes then discard the vanilla.

2. Pour the milk into the top of a double boiler over gently simmering water. Beat in the eggs, egg yolks and sugar and continue to stir over a low heat until the custard thickens. Pour into a bowl, sprinkle with sugar and leave to cool.

3. Spread the trifle sponges with jam and arrange in the base of a serving bowl. Sprinkle with the macaroons. Spoon over the sherry and leave to stand for 1 hour.

4. Pour the custard over the top. Whip the cream until just stiff and spoon over the custard. Decorate with the toasted almonds.

Serves 4-6

9 Summer Pudding with Chantilly Cream

Ingredients

6 large slices stale white bread
50 g/2 oz/¼ cup butter or margarine
100 g/4 oz/½ cup caster sugar
75 ml/5 tbsp water
750 g/1½ lb mixed summer fruits such as raspberries,
strawberries, blackcurrants
150 ml/¼ pt/⅔ cup double cream
½ egg white
15 ml/1 tbsp icing sugar
Few drops of vanilla essence

Method

1. Cut the crusts from the bread, spread with the butter or margarine and cut into fingers. Reserve enough to make a layer in the centre of the pudding and cover the top. Arrange the remaining slices, butter side out, in a pudding basin, pressing them together to line the basin completely.

2. Dissolve the sugar in the water over a low heat. Add the fruits and simmer for about 10 minutes until soft. Spoon half the hot mixture into the bread-lined basin. Make a layer of bread on the top then add the remaining fruit and top with the remaining bread slices.

3. Cover the basin with a saucer, weigh down with a few tins or a heavy weight, leave to cool then refrigerate overnight.

4.   To make the cream, whip the cream and egg whites separately until stiff. Gradually fold them together with the icing sugar and vanilla essence. Chill.

5.   Turn the pudding out on to a serving plate and serve with the chantilly cream.

Serves 4

10 | Crusty Lemon Bake

Ingredients

175 g/6 oz/1½ cups sifted flour
175 g/6 oz/1½ cups margarine or butter
175 g/6 oz/1½ cups sugar
2 eggs
50 g/2 oz/½ cup caster sugar
Juice and rind of 1 large lemon

Method

1.   Melt the margarine and beat in the sugar and eggs. Stir in the flour and turn into a greased pie dish. Bake at 200°C/400°F/gas mark 6 for 15 minutes until golden.

2.   Mix the lemon juice and caster sugar and spread on top of the hot sponge bake. Leave for 5 minutes and serve.

Serves 4 - 6

Apple Fritters

Fritters were once an essential part of the English diet. They are quick to prepare and the crunchy coating with the soft spicy centre, preferably served with lashings of cream, is a filling dessert.

Ingredients

> 3 cooking apples, peeled and cored
> Juice of 1 lemon
> 75 g/3 oz/⅓ cup caster sugar
> 100 g/4 oz/1 cup flour
> 2 eggs
> 25 g/1 oz melted butter
> 150 ml/¼ pt/⅔ cup milk
> 45 ml/3 tbsp water
> 15 ml/1 tsp cinnamon
> Oil for frying

Method

1. Keep the apples in water and half the lemon juice until required.

2. Place the flour in a bowl and add the eggs. Beat together with the milk and add the water. Continue beating and add the melted butter.

3. Cut the apples into rings and dry on a tea towel. Squeeze over the lemon juice and dip in the batter so that each ring is completely coated.

4. Drop each fritter into boiling oil and allow to fry for 2-3 minutes until brown and crispy on the edges. Drain on kitchen paper.

5.   Mix the remaining sugar with the cinnamon and dip the fritter into it immediately it is removed from the oil.

Serves 4-6

12 | Sussex Puddle

Ingredients

> 1 lemon
> 225 g/8 oz/l cup sugar
> 225 g/8 oz/2 cups flour
> 225 g/8 oz/2 cups sultanas
> 100 g/4 oz/½ cup suet
> Pinch salt

Method

1.   Mix the flour, suet and salt with enough water to make a stiff dough. Roll to 5mm/¼″ thick and line a pudding basin, leaving one-third for the top.

2.   Score deep lines all over the lemon and place in the basin. Pack the space around the lemon with the sultanas and sugar. Top with the remaining pastry. Cover with greaseproof paper and steam for 4 hours. Serve with Strawberry sauce (see page 135).

Serves 4

13 Baked Apple Dumplings

Dumplings of all types were once a customary dish for cold November days and often served at shooting parties. The piping hot, sweet smell of apple dumplings brings the full flavour of late autumn warmth to your table. This recipe is made with spicy shortcrust pastry instead of suet crust and is best served with thick, creamy custard. The dumplings can also be eaten cold with clotted cream.

Ingredients

4 cooking apples, peeled and cored
450 g/1 lb shortcrust pastry
75 g/3 oz/⅓ cup caster sugar
5 ml/1 tsp nutmeg
Milk or egg to glaze pastry

Method

1. Divide the pastry into pieces and roll each into a round large enough to enclose an apple. Sprinkle the pastry evenly with a little nutmeg.

2. Place an apple in the centre of the pastry and fill the cored out centre with sugar. Moisten the edges of the pastry with water and gather the edges together firmly, to seal.

3. Turn the dumplings over and brush the tops with milk. Sprinkle caster sugar over and decorate with pastry leaves from the trimmings.

4. Bake at 375°F/190°C/gas mark 5 for 35 minutes until the pastry is golden brown and the apples are soft.

Serves 4

14 Chestnut Pudding

The rich, creamy pudding can look elaborate by garnishing with extra fruits, for a dinner party. It is ideal for Christmas instead of the usual Plum Pudding.

Ingredients

30 Chestnuts
5 eggs
100 g/4 oz/½ cup sugar
5 ml/1 tsp vanilla essence
300 ml/½ pint/1¼ cups cream
1 wineglass sherry
50 g/2 oz candied peel, chopped
100 g/4 oz currants
50 g/2 oz glace cherries, chopped

Method

1. Cut a ring round the chestnuts and put in a saucepan. Cover with water and boil for 15-20 minutes until they are soft. Remove the shells and inner brown skins and pound until smooth

2. Separate the eggs and put the yolks, sugar and vanilla essence in a saucepan over a low heat. Stir until the sauce thickens and remove from the heat.

3. Blend in the cream, chestnuts, sherry, peel, currants and cherries.

4. Beat the whites until stiff and blend into the mixture. Put into a mould and freeze for 4-5 hours. Garnish with some whole cooked sugared chestnuts and glace cherries if desired.

Serves 4

Cakes and Biscuits

There are so many English cake and biscuit recipes, it is hard to choose between them. Here is a selection of some of the most popular traditional recipes.

1 Date Tea Bread

Ingredients

225 g/8 oz/2 cups plain flour
100 g/4 oz/½ cup soft brown sugar
Pinch of salt
5 ml/1 tsp mixed spice
5 ml/1 tsp bicarbonate of soda
50 g/2 oz/¼ cup butter or margarine, melted
15 ml/1 tbsp black treacle
150 ml/¼ pt/⅔ cup tea
1 egg, beaten
75 g/3 oz dates, chopped

Method

1. Mix together the flour, sugar, salt, spice and bicarbonate of soda. Stir in the butter, treacle, tea and egg and mix well until smooth. Stir in the dates.

2. Spoon the mixture into a greased 900 g/2 lb loaf tin and bake in a preheated oven at 180°C/350°F/gas mark 4 for 45 minutes. Turn on to a wire rack to cool. Serve sliced and buttered.

Makes 1 x 900 g/2 lb loaf

2 Madeira Cake

Ingredients

175 g/6 oz/⅔ cup butter or margarine
175 g/6 oz/⅔ cup caster sugar
2.5 ml/½ tsp grated lemon rind
5 ml/1 tsp vanilla essence
3 eggs, lightly beaten
100 g/4 oz/1 cup plain flour
100 g/4 oz/1 cup self-raising flour
30 ml/2 tbsp milk

Method

1. Cream the butter, sugar, lemon rind and vanilla essence until light and fluffy. Beat in the eggs then fold in the flours with enough milk to give a soft consistency.

2. Spoon the mixture into a greased and lined 18 cm/7 in cake tin and bake in a preheated oven at 180°C/350°F/gas mark 4 for 20 minutes. Turn out and cool on a wire rack and serve with a glass of Madeira or sherry.

Makes 1 x 18 cm/7 in cake

3 | Vinegar Fruit Cake

Ingredients

225 g/8 oz/1 cup butter or margarine
450 g/1 lb/4 cups plain flour
225 g/8 oz sultanas
100 g/4 oz raisins
100 g/4 oz currants
225 g/8 oz soft brown sugar
5 ml/1 tsp bicarbonate of soda
300 ml/½ pt/1¼ cups milk
45 ml/3 tbsp malt vinegar

Method

1. Rub the butter or margarine into the flour until the mixture resembles breadcrumbs. Stir in the fruit and sugar and make a well in the centre.

2. Mix together the bicarbonate of soda, milk and vinegar. The mixture will froth. Pour it into the dry ingredients and mix together well.

3. Spoon the mixture into a greased 23 cm/9 in cake tin and bake in a preheated oven at 200°C/400°F/gas mark 6 for 30 minutes. Reduce the temperature to 160°C/325°F/gas mark 3 and bake for a further 1½ hours until firm and golden. Leave to cool slightly in the tin then turn on to a wire rack to cool.

Makes 1 x 23 cm/9 in cake

4 Almond Macaroons

Ingredients

1 egg white
Pinch of salt
100 g/4 oz/½ cup caster sugar
50 g/2 oz/½ cup ground almonds
Sheets rice paper
12 split almonds

Method

1. Whisk the egg white and salt until stiff. Fold in the sugar and ground almonds.

2. Spread the rice paper on a greased baking sheet. Drop spoonfuls of the mixture on the rice paper, spaced well apart. Brush the cakes with a little water and top with split almonds. Bake in a preheated oven at 180°C/350°F/gas mark 4 for 15 minutes.

Makes 12 cakes

5 | Eccles Cakes

Ingredients

50 g/2 oz/¼ cup butter or margarine
50 g/2 oz/¼ cup soft brown sugar
225 g/8 oz/1⅓ cups currants
450 g/1 lb puff or flaky pastry
45 ml/3 tbsp sugar

Method

1. Melt the butter and sugar gently over a low heat, stirring well. Remove from the heat and stir in the currants. Leave to cool slightly.

2. Roll out the pastry on a lightly floured surface and cut into 16 circles. Spoon a little of the mixture on to each circle, and fold the edges into the centre, brushing them with a little water so that they seal together.

3. Turn the cakes over and roll them gently with a rolling pin so that they flatten slightly. Cut 3 slits in the top of each one and sprinkle with sugar.

4. Place on a greased baking sheet and bake in a preheated oven at 200°C/400°F/gas mark 6 for 20 minutes until golden.

Makes 15 cakes

6 | Raspberry Muffins

Ingredients

225 g/8 oz/2 cups plain flour
100 g/4 oz/½ cup caster sugar
10 ml/2 tbsp baking powder
2.5 ml/½ tsp salt
200 g/7 oz raspberries
1 egg, lightly beaten
250 ml/8 fl oz/1 cup milk
120 ml/4 fl oz/½ cup vegetable oil

Method

1. Mix the flour, sugar, baking powder and salt. Stir in the raspberries. Make a well in the centre.

2. Mix together the egg, milk and oil, pour into the dry ingredients and gradually stir until all the dry ingredients are mixed in but the mixture is still lumpy.

3. Spoon the mixture into well-greased deep cake tins and bake in a preheated oven at 200°C/400°F/gas mark 6 for 20 minutes until well risen and springy to touch.

Makes about 12 muffins

7 Treacle Scones

Ingredients

225 g/8 oz/2 cups plain flour
10 ml/2 tsp baking powder
2.5 ml/½ tsp cinnamon
50 g/2 oz/¼ cup margarine
25 g/1 oz/2 tbsp caster sugar
25 g/1 oz black treacle
150 ml/¼ pt/⅔ cup milk

Method

1. Sieve the flour, baking powder and cinnamon into a bowl. Rub in the margarine until the mixture resembles breadcrumbs. Stir in the sugar. Stir in the treacle and enough milk to make a soft dough.

2. Roll out the dough to 1 cm/½ in thick on a lightly floured surface. Cut into rounds and arrange on a greased baking sheet.

3. Bake in a preheated oven at 220°C/425°F/gas mark 7 for 10 to 15 minutes. Serve split and buttered on the day they are made.

Serves 4

8 Rich Man's Shortbread

Ingredients

For the base:
275 g/10 oz/2½ cups plain flour
100 g/4 oz/¼ cup caster sugar
225 g/8 oz/1 cup butter or margarine

For the filling:
225 g/8 oz/1 cup butter or margarine
225 g/8 oz/1 cup soft brown sugar
60 ml/4 tbsp golden syrup
400 g/14 oz canned condensed milk
Few drops of vanilla essence

For the topping:
225 g/8 oz plain chocolate

Method

1. To make the base, sift the flour into a bowl, stir in the sugar then rub in the butter or margarine and knead the mixture to a firm dough. Press into the base of a greased swiss roll tin lined with greased kitchen foil.

2. Bake in a preheated oven at 180°C/350°F/gas mark 4 for 35 minutes. Leave in the tin to cool.

3. Put the butter or margarine, brown sugar, syrup and condensed milk into a pan and stir over a low heat until the sugar has melted. Bring to the boil and simmer gently, stirring continuously, for 7 minutes. Remove from the heat, add the vanilla essence and beat the mixture thoroughly. Pour over

the base and leave to cool and set.

4. Melt the chocolate and spread over the surface of the toffee. Leave to set then cut into small squares.

Makes about 36 squares

9 | Come Again Cake

Ingredients

225 g/8 oz/2 cups flour
100 g/4 oz/½ cup margarine
150 ml/4 pint/⅔ cup water
Pinch salt
275 g/10 oz/2½cups mixed fruit
1 egg, beaten
100 g/4 oz/½ cup sugar

Method

1. Put fruit, sugar, margarine and water in a saucepan and simmer for 20 minutes. Allow to cool and add the beaten egg. Gradually stir in the flour. Turn into a greased cake tin and bake for 1¼ hours at 160°C/325°F/gas mark 3.

Serves 4 - 6

10 | Sponge Drops

Soft little dreams of sponge sandwiched with jam and cream to tempt both the child and adults sweet tooth.

Ingredients

3 eggs, beaten
100 g/4 oz/½ cup castor sugar
2.5 ml/½ tsp vanilla essence
100 g/4 oz/1 cup margarine
5 ml/1 tsp baking powder
100 g/4 oz raspberry jam
150 ml/¼ pt/⅔ cup double cream
Icing sugar for dredging
Butter for greasing

Method

1. Grease 2 large baking sheets

2. Put the eggs, sugar and vanilla essence into a bowl over a saucepan of hot water. Beat until the mixture thickens.

3. Remove the bowl from the saucepan and sift in the flour and baking powder.

4. Put the mixture, a teaspoonful at a time, on the greased baking sheet and bake at 190°C/375°F/gas mark 5 for 10 minutes. Remove the drops and allow to cool on a wire rack.

5. Spread half the drops with the jam. Whip the cream and spoon over the jam. Sandwich with another sponge drop and dredge with icing sugar.

Makes 10-12

11 Nut Squares

A delicious accompaniment to nibble with morning coffee or afternoon tea.

Ingredients

75 g/3 oz plain chocolate
50 g/2 oz/¼ cup butter
100 g/4 oz/1 cup castor sugar
2 eggs
5 ml/1 tsp vanilla essence
2.5 ml/½ tsp baking powder
75 g/3 oz/⅔ cup flour
100 g/4 oz/1 cup chopped nuts

Method

1. Melt the chocolate in a saucepan over hot water and stir in the butter.

2. Add the sugar and beat in the eggs, one at a time. Stir in the vanilla essence. Remove the bowl from the saucepan.

3. Mix the baking powder with the flour and add to the mixture. Blend in the nuts.

4. Spread the mixture in a thin layer and bake at 180°C/350°F/gas mark 4 for 12 to 15 minutes. Cut into small squares while still warm.

Sauces and Dressings

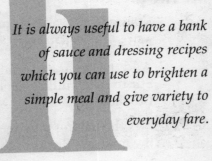

*It is always useful to have a bank
of sauce and dressing recipes
which you can use to brighten a
simple meal and give variety to
everyday fare.*

1 Apple Sauce

Ingredients

450 g/1 lb cooking apples, peeled, cored and sliced
50 g/2 oz/¼ cup sugar
Grated rind and juice of 1 lemon
45 ml/3 tbsp water
30 ml/2 tbsp butter or margarine

Method

1. Place the apples, sugar, lemon rind and water in a saucepan and simmer gently until very soft, stirring occasionally.

2. Purée in a food processor or blender or rub through a sieve.

3. Reheat with the lemon juice and butter until hot and serve with pork, duck or goose.

Serves 4

2 Strawberry Sauce

Ingredients

45 ml/3 tbsp strawberry jam
1 small carton sour cream
300 ml/½ pint/1¼ cups milk

Method

1. Whisk ingredients together in a bowl until fluffy. Pour over spotted dick (see page 110).

Serves 4

3 Bread Sauce

Ingredients

300 ml/½ pt/1¼ cups milk
1 small onion
2 cloves
75 g/3 oz breadcrumbs
15 ml/1 tbsp butter or margarine
Salt and freshly ground black pepper

Method

1. Place the milk in a pan. Stud the onion with the cloves, add to the pan and bring to the boil. Cover and simmer gently for 15 minutes.

2. Strain the milk into the breadcrumbs in a clean pan. Stir in the butter or margarine and season with salt and pepper. Reheat gently without allowing the sauce to boil.

Serves 4

4 Horseradish Sauce

Ingredients

30 ml/2 tbsp fresh horseradish, grated
5 ml/1 tsp caster sugar
10 ml/2 tsp wine vinegar
Pinch of salt
Pinch of mustard powder
150 ml/¼ pt/⅔ cup double cream

Method

1. Mix together the horseradish, sugar, wine vinegar, salt and mustard.

2. Whip the cream until beginning to stiffen then fold in the horseradish mixture. Chill before serving with beef or smoked fish dishes.

Serves 4

5 | Orange Mint Sauce

Ingredients

1 bunch of fresh mint
15 ml/1 tbsp boiling water
10 ml/2 tsp caster sugar
30 ml/2 tbsp white wine vinegar
50 ml/4 tbsp orange juice

Method

1. Chop the mint in a food processor or blender.

2. Add the remaining ingredients and process again until well mixed. Serve with lamb or other rich meats.

Serves 4

6 Salad Dressing

Ingredients

90 ml/3 fl oz/6 tbsp salad oil
2 tbsp wine vinegar
2.5 ml/½ tsp salt
2.5 ml/½ tsp pepper
Pinch dry mustard
Pinch sugar
5 ml/1 tsp freshly chopped herbs

Method

1. Place all the ingredients in a small screw topped jar and shake well until blended.

Serves 4

7 Butterscotch Sauce

Ingredients

30 ml/2 tbsp butter
50 g/2 oz/¼ cup soft brown sugar
15 ml/1 tbsp golden syrup
Juice of 1 lemon

Method

1. Melt the butter and sugar together and bring to the boil for 2 minutes until the mixture is just thickening. Remove from the heat, stir in the lemon juice. Pour over dessert.

Serves 3 - 4

8 Tartare Sauce

Ingredients

150 ml/¼ pt/⅔ cup mayonnaise
15 ml/1 tbsp chopped gherkin
15 ml/1 tbsp chopped fresh parsley
15 ml/1 tbsp chopped capers
15 ml/1 tbsp chopped fresh chives
10 ml/2 tsp lemon juice
Salt and freshly ground black pepper

Method

1. Mix all the ingredients together and season to taste with salt and pepper.

2. Leave to stand for at least 1 hour then check and adjust the seasoning to taste. Serve with fried fish or meat.

Serves 4

9 White Sauce

Ingredients

15 ml/1 tbsp butter or margarine
15 ml/1 tbsp plain flour
300 ml/½ pt/1¼ cups milk
Salt and freshly ground black pepper

Method

1. Melt the butter or margarine in a saucepan, add the flour and cook, stirring, for 1 minute without letting the flour brown.

2. Remove from the heat and stir in the milk.

3. Return to the heat and bring to the boil, stirring continuously, then simmer gently, stirring, for 5 minutes. Season to taste with salt and pepper.

4. *Cheese sauce*: Add 50 g/2 oz grated cheese to the finished sauce and stir until melted.

   Mushroom sauce: Simmer 100 g/4 oz mushrooms in the milk before making the sauce. Chop the mushrooms and add to the finished sauce.

   Onion sauce: Fry 1 sliced onion in the butter or margarine until softened before proceeding with the sauce.

   Parsley sauce: Add some freshly chopped parsley to the finished sauce.

Serves 4

10 Chocolate Sauce

Ingredients

300 ml/½ pt/1¼ cups milk
10 ml/2 tsp cocoa powder
1 egg yolk
15 ml/1 tbsp caster sugar
Few drops of vanilla essence

Method

1. Bring the milk and cocoa to the boil.

2. Beat the egg yolks well with the sugar. Pour the boiling milk on to the egg and sugar mixture, whisking well.

3. Return the mixture to the pan and bring to the boil over a low heat, stirring continuously. Add a few drops of vanilla essence.

Serves 4

11 Traditional Custard

Ingredients

300 ml/½ pt/1¼ cups milk
15 ml/1 tbsp sugar
2 egg yolks, beaten
Few drops of vanilla essence

Method

1. Bring the milk and sugar slowly to the boil.

2. Pour the hot milk on to the beaten egg yolks, stirring continuously. Mix well and return to the saucepan.

3. Stir over a gentle heat for about 5 minutes until the mixture is thick enough to coat the back of a spoon. Stir in the vanilla essence.

Serves 4

12 Raspberry Jam Sauce

Ingredients

75 g/3 oz/⅓ cup sugar
150 ml/¼ pt/⅔ cup water
60 ml/4 tbsp raspberry jam

Method

1. Heat the sugar and water gently until the sugar has dissolved. Bring to the boil and boil rapidly until the mixture forms a syrup.

2.   Stir in the jam until the mixture is smooth then
sieve to remove the pips.

Serves 4

13 Sweet Orange Sauce

Ingredients

> 5 ml/1 tsp cornflour
> 600 ml/1 pt/2½ cups milk
> 1 egg yolk
> Grated rind and juice of 1 orange
> 25 g/1 oz caster sugar

Method

1.   Mix the cornflour with all but 30 ml/2 tbsp of the
milk. Beat the remaining milk with the egg yolk.

2.   Bring the cornflour-milk, orange rind and juice and
sugar to the boil. Remove from the heat and stir in
the egg yolk mixture.

3.   Reheat gently until thick, stirring continuously, but
do not allow the sauce to boil.

Serves 4

14 Gooseberry Sauce

Ingredients

225 g/8 oz gooseberries, cleaned and hulled
15 ml/1 tbsp butter
30 ml/2 tbsp water
5 ml/1 tsp ground cinnamon

Method

1. Place the gooseberries in a saucepan with the water. Bring to the boil and simmer for 10 minutes.

2. Stir in the cinnamon and butter and sweeten if required.

Makes 300 ml/½ pint/1¼ cups

15 Caramel Syrup

Ingredients

100 g/4 oz/1 cup granulated sugar
250 ml/8 fl oz/l cup boiling water
1 tsp vanilla essence

Method

1. Put sugar into a heavy pan and melt, stirring constantly. Bring pan off the heat and stir in the boiling water and vanilla essence. Return to the heat and cook until syrup browns.

Serves 6 - 8

16 Cumberland Sauce

An ideal sauce to serve with hot or cold meats, especially good with venison or roast lamb.

Ingredients

150 ml/¼ pt/⅔ cup stock
10 ml/2 tsp ready-made mustard
150 ml/¼ pt/⅔ cup redcurrant jelly
10 ml/2 tsp olive oil
1 glass port or sherry
1 wineglass orange juice

Method

1. Heat the stock in a saucepan and stir in the mustard and redcurrant jelly.

2. Gradually stir the remaining ingredients and serve when hot.

Makes 300 ml/½ pint/1¼ cups

Preserves
and Drinks

When fruits and vegetables are
in season — cheap and plentiful —
it makes sense to make your own
jams, jellies, chutneys and
pickles to store away for the rest
of the year. They often taste
much better than shop-bought
varieties, and are much cheaper
to make. And what could be
better than such a very special
personal present to a friend or
relative at Christmas?

1 Blackberry and Apple Jam

Ingredients

1 kg/2 lb blackberries
150 ml/¼ pt/⅔ cup water
350 g/12 oz cooking apples, peeled, cored and sliced
1.25 kg/3 lb/6 cups sugar
15 ml/1 tbsp butter or margarine

Method

1. Place the blackberries and half the water in a saucepan and simmer gently until soft.

2. Place the apples and the remaining water in a separate pan and simmer gently until soft. Purée or mash to a pulp.

3. Add the blackberries and sugar to the apple and stir over a low heat until the sugar has dissolved. Add the butter or margarine. Bring to the boil and boil rapidly for about 10 minutes until setting point is reached. A spoonful of cooled jam will wrinkle when pressed.

4. Pour the jam into warmed jars, cover, seal and label.

Makes about 2 kg/4 lb

2 Apple and Mint Jelly

Ingredients

1.5 kg/3 lb cooking apples
Juice of 2 lemons
Bunch of fresh mint
Sugar, warmed

Method

1. Chop the apples roughly, including the peel and cores. Place in a preserving pan and just cover with water. Add the lemon juice and a few sprigs of mint. Bring to the boil and simmer gently until the fruit is soft and pulpy.

2. Pour the pulp into a jelly bag suspended over a large basin and leave to strain for several hours without squeezing the bag.

3. Measure the juice and return it to the preserving pan. Add 450 g/1 lb/2 cups of sugar for each 600 ml/1 pt/2½ cups of juice and 30 ml/2 tbsp of chopped mint and stir over a gentle heat until dissolved. Bring to the boil and boil for about 15 minutes until setting point is reached. A spoonful of cooled jelly will wrinkle when pressed.

Makes about 1.5 kg/3 lb

3 | Orange Marmalade

Ingredients

1.5 kg/3 lb Seville oranges
2 lemons
4 l/7 pts water
3 kg/6 lb preserving sugar

Method

1. Halve the fruit and squeeze the juice. Chop the peel and soak it in 1.5 l/3 pts/7½ cups of the water for 24 hours. Tie the pips in a piece of muslin.

2. Place the peel and soaking water, the remaining water and pips in a preserving pan or large saucepan and simmer for 2 hours until the peel is soft. Discard the pips.

3. Stir in the sugar until dissolved. Bring to the boil and boil for about 25 minutes until setting point is reached. A spoonful of cooled marmalade will wrinkle when pressed.

4. Skim any scum from the top, cool slightly, then pour into warmed jars, cover, seal and label.

Makes 3.2 kg/7 lb

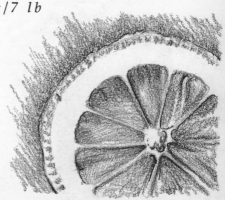

4 Mincemeat

Ingredients

225 g/8 oz/1⅓ cups currants
225 g/8 oz/1⅓ cups sultanas
225 g/8 oz/1⅓ cups raisins
100 g/4 oz/⅔ cup chopped mixed peel
225 g/8 oz cooking apples, peeled, cored and grated
100 g/4 oz/1 cup almonds, chopped
225 g/8 oz/1 cup soft brown sugar
100 g/4 oz/1 cup shredded suet
5 ml/1 tsp nutmeg
5 ml/1 tsp cinnamon
Grated rind and juice of 1 lemon

Method

1. Chop the dried fruit and place in a bowl. Mix with the remaining ingredients and stir thoroughly. Cover the bowl and leave to stand for 2 days, stirring occasionally.

2. Spoon the mincemeat into jars and cover.

Makes 1.5 kg/3½ lb

5 | Pickled Onions

Ingredients

1 1/2 pts/5 cups malt vinegar
1 sachet pickling spices
1 onion, halved
1.25 kg/3 lb pickling onions
225 g/8 oz salt
1.25 l/4 pts/10 cups water

Method

1. Place the vinegar in a saucepan and add the spices and onion. Bring to the boil, cover and simmer for 2 minutes. Leave to stand, covered, for 3 hours. Remove the spices and onion.

2. Dissolve half the salt in half the water. Place the onions in a bowl, pour over the salt water and cover, keeping the onions below the water. Leave to stand for 12 hours.

3. Drain and rinse the onions then peel and trim them and return them to the bowl. Dissolve the remaining salt in the remaining water, pour over the onions, cover and leave to stand for 24 hours.

4. Drain, rinse and pat dry. Pack into jars and pour over the spiced vinegar. Leave to mature for 3 months.

Makes 1.25 kg/3 lb

6 | Pear and Apple Chutney

Ingredients

1 kg/2 lb pears, peeled, cored and diced
1 kg/2 lb apples, peeled, cored and diced
450 g/1 lb onions, chopped
1.2 l/2½ pts/6 cups malt vinegar
450 g/1 lb dates, chopped
15 ml/1 tbsp salt
1 kg/2 lb golden syrup
15 ml/1 tbsp ground ginger
30 ml/2 tbsp mustard powder

Method

1. Place the pears, apples, onions and vinegar in a pan, bring to the boil and simmer gently until tender.

2. Add the remaining ingredients, return to the boil and simmer, uncovered, until thick and golden. Spoon into warmed jars, seal and label.

Makes about 2.5 kg/6 lb

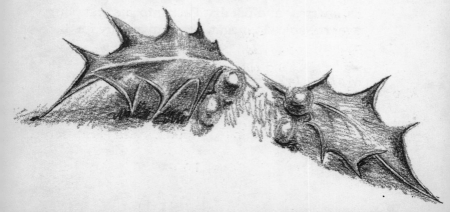

7 Mulled Wine

Ingredients

50 g/2 oz/¼ cup brown sugar
150 ml/¼ pt/⅔ cup water
1 bottle red wine
2 oranges suck with 6 cloves
2 sticks cinnamon
150 ml/¼ pt/⅔ cup brandy

1. Dissolve the sugar in the water over a low heat, stirring continuously.

2. Add the wine, oranges and cinnamon and heat very slowly until almost boiling.

3. Add the brandy and strain into warm glasses. Serve hot.

Serves 6

8 Lemon Cordial

Ingredients

2 lemons
1 kg/2 lb/8 cups sugar
50 g/2 oz citric acid
900 ml/1½ pints water

Method

1. Boil water, thinly peeled lemon rind and sugar for 1 hour. Strain. Stir in the lemon juice and acid. Bottle.

Makes 1.2 l/2 pts/5 cups

9 | Traditional Lemon Squash

Ingredients

6 lemons
2 kg/4 lb/6 cups granulated sugar
1.5 l/2½ pts/6 cups water
25 g/1 oz/2 tbsp citric acid

Method

1. Grate the rind and squeeze the juice from the lemons.

2. Bring the lemon rind, sugar and water to the boil and simmer for 10 minutes. Leave to cool.

3. Add the lemon juice and citric acid, strain into bottles and dilute to taste.

Makes 1.2 l/2 pts/5 cups

10 | Cinnamon Tea

Ingredients

Pot of tea
7½ cm/3˝ cinnamon stick
30 ml/6 tsp Grand Marnier

Method

1. Add the cinnamon to the tea. Leave to stand and pour out. Add 2 teaspoons Grand Marnier to each cup.

Serves 3

Index

Almonds
  Almond Macaroons........................ 126
Angels on Horseback 19
Appetisers
  Angels on Horseback 19
  Buttered Mussels 18
  Devilled Ham Toasts...................... 22
  Soft Roes with Bacon................. 20–21
  Two-Cheese Pots 17
  Whitebait....................................... 23
Apples
  Apple Fritters 118–119
  Apple and Mint Jelly 148
  Apple Sauce.................................... 135
  Baked Apple Dumplings.............. 120
  Blackberry and Apple Jam 147
  Pear and Apple Chutney.............. 152
  Pork with Apple and Honey.... 76–77
  Sausage and Apple Yorkshires...... 75
Aubergine
  Baked Vegetables with Cheese 84–85
Autumn Goose..................................... 50

Bacon
  Bacon Roly Poly 72
  Bean and Bacon Hot Pot 77
  Leek and Bacon Toastie 98
  Liver and Bacon 71
  Smoked Bacon Rolls 81
  Soft Roes with Bacon................. 20–21
Baked Vegetables with Cheese ... 84–85
Bakewell Tart..................................... 107
Beans
  Lamb and Beans.............................. 80
  Bean and Bacon Hot Pot 77
Beef
  Beef in Beer 62
  Beef Fillet in Sherry Sauce 65
  Beef and Ham Roll.......................... 55
  Beef Pot Roast................................. 63
  Beef Wellington.......................... 56–57
  Crispy-Topped Mince Pies............. 64
  Oxtail Soup 11
  Roast Beef and Yorkshire
    Pudding.................................. 60–61
  Steak and Kidney Pie 58–59
Beetroot
  Baked Beetroot with
    Soured Cream................................ 93
Biscuits *see* Cakes and Biscuits

Blackberries
  Blackberry and Apple Jam 147
Blackcurrants
  Summer Pudding with Chantilly
    Cream 116–117
Bread and Butter Pudding 108
Bread Sauce 136
Broccoli
  Broccoli in Lemon Sauce................. 94
Bubble and Squeak 57

Cakes and Biscuits
  Almond Macaroons........................ 126
  Cut and Come Again Cake 131
  Date Tea Bread............................... 123
  Eccles Cakes................................... 127
  Madeira Cake 124
  Nut Squares 133
  Raspberry Muffins......................... 128
  Rich Man's Shortbread.......... 130–131
  Sponge Drops................................. 132
  Treacle Scones 129
  Vinegar Fruit Cake 125
Carrots
  Carrots with Mint and Lemon....... 95
Cinnamon Carrots 101
Celery
  Celery Bake..................................... 96
Chantilly Cream
  Summer Pudding with Chantilly
    Cream 116–117
Cheese
  Baked Vegetables with Cheese 84–85
  Cheese Pasties 90
  Cheese Sauce 140
  Cheese Straws 91
  Cheese Tarts 89
  Chicken and Stilton Rolls 45
  Deep Fried Cheese Balls 88–89
  Pan Haggerty 99
  Soldiers Sandwich 86
  Two-Cheese Pots 17
  Welsh Rarebit 83
Chestnuts
  Chestnut Pudding 121
Chicken
  Chicken with Leek and Watercress
    Sauce.. 40–41
  Chicken with Parsley
    Dumplings.................................. 42–43

Chicken and Stilton Rolls 45
Cock-a-Leekie Soup 10
English Pottage 15
Gardener's Chicken 39
Pork and Chicken Layer Pie..... 78–79
Spicy Chicken 47
Chocolate
  Chocolate Sauce 141
Chutney
  Pear and Apple Chutney 152
Cider Syllabub.................................. 113
Cock-a-Leekie Soup........................... 10
Coffee Fudge Pudding..................... 109
Courgettes
  Stuffed Courgettes............................ 97
Crab
  Crab Pie.. 30
  Crab Salad 25
Crispy-Topped Mince Pies................ 64
Crown Roast of Lamb 68–69
Cumberland Sauce 145
Custard
  Traditional Custard 142
Cut and Come Again Cake 131

Dates
  Date Tea Bread 123
Deep Fried Cheese Balls 88–89
Desserts
  Apple Fritters 118–119
  Baked Apple Dumplings............... 120
  Bakewell Tart................................... 107
  Bread and Butter Pudding 108
  Chestnut Pudding 121
  Cider Syllabub................................. 113
  Coffee Fudge Pudding................... 109
  English Trifle 115
  Gooseberry Fool.............................. 114
  Queen of Puddings......................... 112
  Spotted Dick with Rum
  Sauce.. 110–111
  Summer Pudding with
  Chantilly Cream...................... 116–117
  Sussex Puddle 119
  Sweet Omelettes................................ 87
Devilled Ham Toasts.......................... 22
Devilled Kidneys 73
Dressings and Sauces
  Apple Sauce 135
  Bread Sauce 136
  Chocolate Sauce 141
  Cumberland Sauce 145
  Horseradish Sauce 137
  Orange Mint Sauce 137
  Raspberry Jam Sauce..................... 142

Sweet Orange Sauce 143
Tartare Sauce 139
Traditional Custard 142
White Sauce 140
Drinks
  Cinnamon Tea 154
  Lemon Cordial 153
  Mulled Wine 153
  Traditional Lemon Squash 154
Duck
  Duck in Port................................ 46–47
Dumplings
  Baked Apple Dumplings............... 120
  Chicken with Parsley Dumplings.
  42–43
  Lentil Stew with Dumplings........ 102

Eccles Cakes..................................... 127
Edwardian Game........................... 52–53
Eel
  Eel and Green Peas 37
Eggs
  Deep Fried Cheese Balls 88–89
  Sweet Omelettes................................ 87
English Pottage 15
English Trifle 115

Fish
  Baked Mackerel with Mustard 36
  Eel and Green Peas 37
  Herrings in Oatmeal........................ 31
  Kedgeree 27
  Lemon Fish Casserole 35
  Soft Roes with Bacon................. 20–21
  Steamed Sole in Cheese Sauce . 32–33
  Tomato Fish Pie 28–29
  Whitebait... 23
Fools
  Gooseberry Fool.............................. 114
Fritters
  Apple Fritters 118–119
Fruit Cakes
  Vinegar Fruit Cake 125

Game
  Duck in Port................................ 46–47
  Edwardian Game....................... 52–53
  Jugged Hare...................................... 44
  Pigeon Casserole 49
  Rabbit Pie 48
  Rabbit Soup 16
  Venison with Redcurrant Sauce 51
Gardener's Chicken............................ 39
Goose
  Autumn Goose................................. 50

Gooseberries
Gooseberry Fool.............................. 114

Ham
Beef and Ham Roll........................... 55
Devilled Ham Toasts....................... 22
Honey Roast Ham 74
Pea and Ham Soup 12
Hare
Jugged Hare..................................... 44
Roast Hare 41
Hash
North of England Hash 67
Herrings
Herrings in Oatmeal....................... 31
Honey Roast Ham 74
Horseradish Sauce............................. 137

Jam
Blackberry and Apple Jam 147
Raspberry Jam Sauce..................... 144
Jugged Hare.. 44

Kedgeree 27
Kidneys
Devilled Kidneys 73
Steak and Kidney Pie 58–59

Lamb
Crown Roast of Lamb 68–69
Devilled Kidneys 73
Lamb and Beans............................... 80
Liver and Bacon 71
North of England Hash 67
Roast Lamb with Nut and Apricot
Stuffing.. 70
Leeks
Chicken with Leek and Watercress
Sauce.. 40–41
Cock-a-Leekie Soup......................... 10
Leek and Bacon Toastie 98
Lemons
Broccoli in Lemon Sauce................. 94
Crusty Lemon Bake 117
Lemon Fish Casserole 35
Traditional Lemon Squash 154
Lentils
Lentil Stew with Dumplings........ 102
Liver
Liver and Bacon 71
Lobster
Grilled Lobster 26

Macaroons
Almond Macaroons....................... 126

Mackerel
Baked Mackerel with Mustard 36
Madeira Cake 124
Marmalade
Orange Marmalade 149
Mince
Beef and Ham Roll........................... 55
Crispy-Topped Mince Pies............. 64
Mincemeat 150
Muffins
Raspberry Muffins......................... 128
Mulled Wine...................................... 153
Mushrooms
Mushroom Sauce 140
Mussels
Buttered Mussels 18
Mussels with Saffron............... 34–35
North of England Hash 67
Nuts
Almond Macaroons....................... 126
Chestnut Pudding 121
Nut Squares 133
Roast Lamb with Nut and Apricot
Stuffing.. 70

Omelettes
Sweet Omelettes............................... 87
Onions
Baked Onions 103
Onion Sauce................................... 140
Pickled Onions 151
Oranges
Cider Syllabub................................ 113
Orange Marmalade 149
Orange Mint Sauce 138
Sweet Orange Sauce 143
Oxtail
Oxtail Soup 11
Oysters
Angels on Horseback 19

Pan Haggerty 99
Parsley
Chicken with Parsley
Dumplings................................. 42–43
Parsley Sauce................................. 140
Parsnips
Creamed Parsnips........................... 104
Partridge
Edwardian Game....................... 52–53
Pea and Ham Soup 12
Pear and Apple Chutney 152
Peas
Eel and Green Peas......................... 37
Pea and Ham Soup 12

Pheasant
Edwardian Game........................ 52–53
Pickled Onions 151
Pigeon
Pigeon Casserole................................ 49
Pork
Bacon Roly Poly 72
Beef and Ham Roll........................... 55
Devilled Ham Toasts....................... 22
Honey Roast Ham 74
Leek and Bacon Toastie 98
Liver and Bacon 71
Pea and Ham Soup.......................... 12
Pork with Apple and Honey.... 76–77
Pork and Chicken Layer Pie..... 78–79
Sausage and Apple Yorkshires...... 75
Smoked Bacon Rolls 81
Soft Roes with Bacon................. 20–21
Potatoes
Pan Haggerty 99
Poultry
Autumn Goose................................... 50
Chicken with Leek and Watercress
Sauce.. 40–41
Chicken with Parsley Dumplings ...
42–43
Chicken and Stilton Rolls 45
Cock-a-Leekie Soup.......................... 10
Duck in Port................................. 46–47
English Pottage................................. 15
Gardener's Chicken 39
Pork and Chicken Layer Pie..... 78–79
Preserves
Apple and Mint Jelly...................... 148
Blackberry and Apple Jam 147
Mincemeat 150
Orange Marmalade 149
Pear and Apple Chutney 152
Pickled Onions 151
Puddings
Apple Fritters 118–119
Baked Apple Dumplings............... 120
Bakewell Tart................................... 107
Bread and Butter Pudding 108
Chestnut Pudding 121
Cider Syllabub................................. 113
Coffee Fudge Pudding................... 109
English Trifle 115
Gooseberry Fool.............................. 114
Queen of Puddings......................... 112
Spotted Dick with Rum
Sauce.. 110–111
Summer Pudding with Chantilly
Cream 116–117
Sweet Omelettes............................... 87

Pulses
Eel and Green Peas............................ 37
Lamb and Beans................................. 80
Lentil Stew with Dumplings........ 102
Pea and Ham Soup............................ 12

Queen of Puddings........................... 112

Rabbit
Jugged Rabbit.................................... 44
Rabbit Pie... 48
Rabbit Soup 16
Raspberries
Raspberry Jam Sauce...................... 144
Raspberry Muffins........................... 128
Summer Pudding with
Chantilly Cream................... 116–117
Rich Man's Shortbread............. 130–131
Roast Beef
Roast Beef and Yorkshire
Pudding.................................... 60–61
Roast Lamb
Crown Roast of Lamb 68–69
Roast Lamb with Nut and
Apricot Stuffing 70

Sauces and Dressings
Apple Sauce..................................... 135
Bread Sauce 136
Butterscotch Sauce 138
Caramel Syrup 144
Chocolate Sauce 141
Cumberland Sauce 145
Gooseberry Sauce 144
Horseradish Sauce 137
Orange Mint Sauce 137
Raspberry Jam Sauce...................... 142
Salad Dressing 138
Strawberry Suace 135
Sweet Orange Sauce 143
Tartare Sauce 139
Traditional Custard 142
White Sauce 140
Sausages
Sausage and Apple Yorkshires...... 75
Savoury Crumble 61
Scones
Treacle Scones 129
Seafood
Angels on Horseback 19
Baked Mackerel with Mustard 36
Buttered Mussels 18
Crab Pie 30
Crab Salad... 25
Eel and Green Peas............................ 37

Grilled Lobster 26
Herrings in Oatmeal........................ 31
Kedgeree 27
Mussels with Saffron.................. 34–35
Seafood Flan 33
Soft Roes with Bacon................. 20–21
Steamed Sole in Cheese Sauce . 32–33
Tomato Fish Pie 28–29
Whitebait... 23
Shortbread
  Rich Man's Shortbread.......... 130–131
Soft Roes with Bacon...................... 20–21
Soldiers Sandwich 86
Sole
  Steamed Sole in Cheese Sauce . 32–33
Soups
  Cock-a-Leekie Soup.......................... 10
  English Pottage 15
  Oxtail Soup....................................... 11
  Pea and Ham Soup........................... 12
  Rabbit Soup 16
  Tomato and Barley Soup 13
  Watercress Soup 21
  Winter Vegetable Soup 14
Spicy Chicken 47
Sponge Drops..................................... 132
Spotted Dick with Rum
  Sauce... 110–111
Squash
  Traditional Lemon Squash 154
Steak and Kidney Pie 58–59
Strawberries
Summer Pudding with Chantilly
  Cream 116–117
Summer Pudding with Chantilly
  Cream 116–117
Sweets *see* Desserts
Syllabub
  Cider Syllabub................................ 113

Tartare Sauce..................................... 139

Tomatoes
  Tomato and Barley Soup 13
  Tomato Fish Pie 28–29
Treacle Scones 129
Trifle
  English Trifle 115
Turnips
  Turnips in Cheese Sauce............... 105
Two-Cheese Pots 17

Vegetables
  Baked Beetroot with Soured
    Cream 93
  Baked Onions 103
  Baked Vegetables with Cheese 84–85
  Broccoli in Lemon Sauce................. 94
  Carrots with Mint and Lemon....... 95
  Celery Bake 96
  Cock-a-Leekie Soup.......................... 10
  Creamed Parsnips.......................... 104
  English Pottage 15
  Leek and Bacon Toastie 98
  Pan Haggerty 99
  Pea and Ham Soup.......................... 12
  Stuffed Courgettes.......................... 97
  Turnips in Cheese Sauce............... 105
  Vegetable Hot Pot................. 100–101
  Winter Vegetable Soup 14
Venison
  Venison with Redcurrant Sauce 51
Vinegar Fruit Cake 125

Watercress Soup 21
Welsh Rarebit..................................... 83
White Sauce 140
Whitebait... 23
Wine
  Mulled Wine.................................. 153
Winter Vegetable Soup 14

Yorkshire Pudding 60–61

Opening doors to the World of books

BOOK TOKEN

Book Tokens

Book Tokens can be bought and exchanged at most bookshops